D0122319

STUDIES IN HISTORY, ECONOMICS, AND PUBLIC LAW

EDITED BY THE FACULTY OF POLITICAL SCIENCE
OF COLUMBIA UNIVERSITY

Number 281

# CONSULAR PRIVILEGES AND IMMUNITIES

# CONSULAR PRIVILEGES AND IMMUNITIES

BY

IRVIN STEWART

AMS PRESS
NEW YORK

COLUMBIA UNIVERSITY
STUDIES IN THE
SOCIAL SCIENCES

281

The Series was formerly known as
*Studies in History, Economics and Public Law.*

Reprinted with the permission of Columbia University Press
From the edition of 1926, New York
First AMS EDITION published 1968
Manufactured in the United States of America

Library of Congress Catalogue Card Number: 68-57583

AMS PRESS, INC.
NEW YORK, N.Y. 10003

# PREFACE

THE aim of this monograph is to present a study of a narrow field rather than a survey of a broad one. The term " consular privileges and immunities " has been construed to apply to those exceptions from the ordinary operation of municipal law which relate specifically to the consular office; and those which any national of the consul's state might enjoy have been excluded. No attempt has been made to treat consular organization or functions; and no consideration has been given the anomalous situation in certain states where extraterritorial privileges have been granted.

In the course of time two sets of consular privileges and immunities have developed: one for the consular officer who is a national of the appointing state and who is engaged in no pursuit other than the consular occupation; and a second, more limited, group for other consular officers. As consular services have increased in size and importance, there has been a steady increase in the qualifications prerequisite to entrance into them, until today it is believed that most important consular offices are filled by nationals who engage in none other than the consular business. The present study is confined to the privileges and immunities of this class of consular officials.

It is a pleasure to acknowledge obligations under which the author has been placed in the preparation of this study. Professor Charles G. Haines, formerly of the University of Texas and now of the Southern Branch of the University of California, was instrumental in creating an interest in the subject and has been of assistance in many ways. Professors Charles Cheney Hyde and Joseph P. Chamberlain of Columbia University have rendered invaluable service through their suggestions and criticisms. The author is indebted to the Honorable Wilbur J. Carr, Assistant Secretary of State of the United States, for permission to consult certain records; and to the Bureau of Indexes and Archives of the Department of State, and particularly the Chief thereof, for unfailing consideration and courtesy while those records were being consulted. The Assistant Director of the Pan-American Union and the Librarian of the Columbus Memorial Library made available a large amount of material; and many foreign consular officers stationed in the United States have aided by calling attention to sources which otherwise might have been overlooked.

Without the assistance which has been rendered by these several individuals, the present monograph would have been impossible; but for opinions expressed and method of handling material, the author alone bears the responsibility.

# CONTENTS

PAGE

CHAPTER I



CHAPTER II



CHAPTER III



CHAPTER IV



CHAPTER V



CHAPTER VI

# CHAPTER I

## The Public Character of Consuls

For a complete understanding of the legal position of consuls at least four, and possibly five, sources of authority must be consulted: viz., the laws and executive regulations of the state which appoints the consul, those of the state which grants him his exequatur, treaties in force between the two states, and the general customs and usages applicable to the subject. To these may be added for the sake of completeness, doctrine as established in the writings of international jurists.

The first of these, the laws and regulations of the state granting the patent, primarily applies between the consul and his government. The consular regulations of many states expressly provide that the consul has no diplomatic character and forbid the invoking of the privileges of diplomatic agents. While such a provision directly concerns only the claims which may be put forward by the consuls appointed by the particular state, it may be taken as a fairly certain indication that the same rule will be applied to consuls whom that state may receive.

Of more importance in the determination of the public character of a consul is the law of the state which receives him. While no state may change the rules of international law, a state may establish a basis in municipal law for a right secured by international law; and it may grant privileges beyond those which international law requires. Naturally this makes it possible for the extent of the immunities to vary with the different states since it could hardly be expected that all states would enact the same law. In actual practice only a few states have made any attempt to place on a definite basis the privileges which foreign consuls within their limits may enjoy; the majority have been content to let the matter rest on usage so far as treaty provisions do not cover the situation.

Of greater importance than either of the foregoing because of their wider extent are the provisions inserted in general treaties or incorporated into consular conventions. These again have introduced an element of confusion into the general situation in almost exact proportion as they have cleared up the particular one; for the treaties are applicable only as between the parties signatory, and there is no general consular convention in effect. Since the extent of the immunities granted in the different treaties has varied, and since the states of the world have not negotiated conventions at the same rate, some being laggard in this respect while others have been exceedingly active, the difficulty of expressing in general formulae the extent of consular privileges and the consequent definition of the consular character has increased. Fortunately, practically all of the more recent conventions have approached a norm; and as the use of the most-favored-nation clause is more widely extended, the degree of uniformity is steadily becoming greater. Of course, when there is an applicable treaty provision it takes precedence over the general rules of international law and, by express stipulation, over the provisions of the local law.

Much has been left to custom in this field; and as custom in the various consular districts has not been the same, it is impossible to state definitely in a single work everything that may be claimed in a particular place on this ground. Nevertheless, certain outstanding privileges may be claimed on the basis of usage; and in the absence of treaties or positive law, custom is considered as controlling. Much that formerly was based on custom has been incorporated into treaties; and conversely, much that has been written into treaties has been advocated by some authors as having a basis of custom, in cases where there are no governing treaty provisions.

The extent to which international doctrine is applicable is doubtful. Properly its position is prophetic, not descriptive or historical. Much unnecessary confusion has been introduced into the subject by writers and even statesmen and jurists through their failure to distinguish between what exists and what in their opinion, or in that of some one else, should exist. Text writers have shown themselves prone to copy each other, probably as the easiest way to treat an unsatisfactory field; what one man says ought to be the rule governing consular privileges passes through the hands of several writers and finally emerges as a statement that such does exist; and that without other authority cited than the first statement. Yet the important part that may be played by doctrine is not to be denied. By pointing out what should be the rule, it helps to focus attention upon an existing lacuna and paves the way for the eventual acceptance of a new rule.[1]

From the above it is apparent that the extent to which consular privileges are recognized may be by no means uniform in all states. Such is the case. At one extreme is England which has steadily refused to negotiate a single consular convention and which has challenged the existence of certain privileges based upon custom; at the other is

[1] On the subject of the factors to be considered in determining the legal condition of consuls see an article by Dr. Daniel Antokoletz on "La Condición Jurídica de los Cónsules y Especialmente de los Cónsules Argentinos" in *Revista Diplomática y Consular Argentina,* December, 1915, vol. i, no. 2.

France, which has negotiated a large number of such treaties, and has been ready to extend broad privileges even in the absence of treaty stipulations. Between the two positions fall the other states, their practice being far from uniform. Thus it is necessary to examine the position of the particular state to ascertain just what privileges a consul may claim.

The extent to which these privileges have been recognized has varied not only from state to state but also within particular states from time to time. Consequently, the problem of determining the exact scope of consular exemptions and of stating the present position of each of the more important states on each of these is no small one; and the uncertainty which results is fraught with the possibility of international misunderstanding and friction.[1]

[1] In view of the opposing stands taken by text writers reflecting the frequently conflicting positions of the various governments, the statement made by Borel is interesting:

"... If the prerogatives of consuls have not been specified in the modern treaties which have been negotiated between the sovereigns of Europe, it is because they are too well known for it to be thought necessary to give them an ulterior designation. For, these same princes have taken care to express them in the conventions which they have made with the less enlightened powers, as with the Barbary States and with the Ottoman Porte." (Borel, Francoise, *De l'Origine et des Fonctions des Consuls.*)

Proof of the statement in the text, which of course is in direct opposition to the quotation from Borel is to be found in a report presented to the Congress of the Republic of Colombia by the secretary of foreign relations in 1847. In pointing out the extremely unsatisfactory position of foreign consuls in the Republic, the secretary said:

"The poorly defined consular prerogatives which are found; the pretension, if not explicit at least implied, of the governments of France and Great Britain to obtain for their consuls and vice consuls in Spanish America the same immunities which they have secured for those whom they send to the coasts of Africa; and the absence of categorical declarations in our laws, are the causes which give rise to daily contests which afterwards pressed and circulated almost always end only because the official who represents the Republic must yield, leaving his honor impaired, or resolve to charge himself with the enormous responsibility of

At the outset of a discussion of the character of the consular office one encounters the question: Are consuls diplomatic agents and as such entitled to the privileges and immunities which inhere in that character? If the question be answered in the affirmative, the problem is reduced to that of ascertaining what exemptions these officers enjoy. If it be answered in the negative, there is still the problem of determining whether or not they are, nevertheless, entitled to some privileges; and if so, what these are. Much has been written on the general subject. It is the purpose of the present chapter to present the results of an examination of the official declarations of a number of states.

Three distinct answers to the question have been given, and on the basis of these answers the writers on the subject may be divided into three groups. At one extreme is a small group of publicists, headed by Pinheiro-Ferreira, which maintains that consuls are public ministers, though perhaps

having involved his country in a troublesome question which exposes the national dignity to greater outrages.

"This state of things, and principally the cause from which it springs merits very serious consideration.

"No other point of the law of nations has been treated by its expositors with such lightness and vagueness, as that of the privileges of consuls. While some assert that these functionaries lack all immunity, that they are denied other guarantees than those owed to any transient foreigner vested with a safe conduct, and finally that they have no character superior to that of mere commercial agents; other writers, and among them the celebrated Vattel, maintain that consuls represent the Government which names them, that they are not subject to the jurisdiction of the country in which they reside, and that they cannot be subjected to it except in case of having committed atrocious crimes.

"It results from this disagreement of opinions and doctrines that, if the matter were not exceedingly important and delicate to leave abandoned to chance, a weak state should not adopt, because it could not do so with assurance of success any decisive determination on this point; since whatever it might be, it would be resisted, not only by force, but also with the arms of reason and the authority of the peso." (Uribe, *Anales Diplomáticos y Consulares de Colombia*, vol. iii, pp. 193-197.)

of a grade lower than chargés d'affaires.[1] The opposite view is that consuls are mere commercial agents, and as such entitled to no different treatment than other foreigners. The third view is a compromise between the two preceding, refusing to recognize consuls as entitled to the character and privileges of public ministers but conceding that they are in spite of that fact, entitled to certain exemptions, that they are to a certain extent under the protection of the law of nations. It is this last view which has the support of the majority of the publicists of today, and what is more important, the sanction of the statements and practice of modern governments.

The difficulty in the position is in determining just what is the degree of protection to which the consuls are entitled; and it is to this problem that the present study is addressed. The statement usually found is that though consuls are not public ministers, they enjoy those exemptions which are essential to the discharge of their functions. As established by treaties, by law, or by usage the principal exemptions relate to the consular archives; the placing of insignia over the consulate and the inviolability of the latter; the taxation of consuls; the consul's relation to the local justice; and his exemption from military billeting, military service, and public service; together with a few subjects of lesser importance. Each of these will be taken up in its turn in an endeavor to establish its scope; but first comes a consideration of the

[1] The chief exponents of this position in addition to Pinheiro-Ferreira, are Steck, de Cussy, Moreuil, and de Clerq and de Vallet. M. Engelhardt has shown himself on ardent champion of this view at several sessions of the Institute of International Law. His various reports on the subject of consular immunities present an excellent exposition of the reasons for the position. The International Law Association at its meeting in Buenos Aires in 1922 passed without discussion a resolution pointing out the desirability of granting to consuls of career the largest prerogatives of diplomatic agents. Report of the Thirty-first Conference, p. 168.

position of the several states on the general character of the consular office.

A survey of the pertinent publications of a number of states shows that the majority have unreservedly placed themselves in opposition to the view that consuls are public ministers, though in nearly every case there is no doubt that the consul is regarded as being entitled to more consideration than an ordinary national of his state. No reference is made to statements of text writers, nor are treaties listed below—though it is believed that a study of treaties of other states would show results similar to those of a study of United States treaties. Of the latter only two consider the question of the similarity between consular and diplomatic positions, and both of those specifically deny the existence of any diplomatic character on the part of consuls. The other three sources have been used: laws and regulations of sending and receiving states and custom where reference to it has been found.

*Argentina:* "They are, in a foreign country, under the special protection of the law of nations, and must claim all the immunities and privileges accorded to their class." *Reglamento Consular,* 1862, Art. 9 contained in *Memoria del Ministerio de Relaciones Esteriores* for 1879. This statement is repeated in Article 58 of the *Reglamento Consular* of 1906 and is followed in Article 59 by the declaration: "According to international law, a consular officer has no representative or diplomatic character with respect to the country in which he is accredited. He has, notwithstanding, a representative character in that which refers to the commercial interests of the country which has accredited him." The *Anuario* of the Ministry of Foreign Relations for 1908 contains an extract from a study by Dr. Carlos Alfredo Becú, secretary of the Argentine delegation at The Hague conferences. Among other things, the author, apparently with the approval of the Ministry, states: "Consuls, mere commercial agents, are not invested with diplomatic character. . . . Their powers spring from their functions, and are only those necessary for their discharge." Page 291.

*Belgium:* A statement of consular concessions made by royal decree in Belgium, set out in a letter of May 19, 1838, to the Secretary of State of the United States, shows them to be far short of those of diplomatic agents, which seems to be proof of a non-recognition of diplomatic character. Dept. of State, MS. Belgium Notes, Vol. I, p. 1.

*Bolivia:* "Consular agents do not enjoy prerogatives except in so far as the customary law of the country in which they function permits; nor do they have an official character to address themselves to the authorities of the place in which they reside." *Reglamento Consular,* 1877, Art. 20. The Regulations of 1887 contain a separate title referring to foreign consuls resident in Bolivia, Article 103 of which is to the effect that "Consuls do not enjoy the exemptions conceded to ministers and diplomatic agents."

*Chile:* Article 35 of the *Reglamento Consular* of 1897: "Consuls cannot claim diplomatic privileges, exemptions, and immunities." The same idea is contained in the Regulations of 1915, Article 112 of which provides that "Consuls lack a political character and cannot, in consequence, be considered as diplomatic officers," with the additional statement that "They find themselves in the foreign country under the protection of the law of nations and must claim the prerogatives accorded to those of their class."

*Colombia:* "They do not have . . . diplomatic character with respect to the country to which they are accredited. Nevertheless, they have a representative character in that which refers to the commercial interests of Colombia." *Guía Consular,* p. 29.

*Costa Rica:* " Consuls cannot claim diplomatic privileges, exemptions, or immunities," nor seek precedence or distinctions not granted by treaties or usage. *Reglamento Consular,* 1888, Art. 29.

*Cuba:* Pages 6 and 7 of the *Instrucciones Provisionales para el Servicio Consular* are almost identical with Article 112 of the Chilean Regulations of 1915.

*Germany:* As early as 1796 Prussia issued regulations to the effect that:

> We will endeavor still to assure to each of them the enjoyment of their immunities, rights, and prerogatives which will be due them in their capacity as consuls. These immunities differing nevertheless according to the countries, we will abstain from establishing here any general principle in this regard, reserving to Ourselves to make known our intention to consuls in each particular and doubtful case of which they will judge it a duty to make a report to us. (Bursotti, *Guide des Agents Consulaires*, vol. ii, p. 274.)

*Great Britain:* " I am also to remind you with reference to the expressions ' Envoy ' and ' Mission,' which repeatedly occur in your despatch, that as Her Majesty's Consul at Massowah, you hold no representative character in Abyssinia." Mr. Murray to Consul Cameron, British and Foreign State Papers, Vol. 53, p. 67 (1863). The central idea of the text is further borne out by the provision in the General Instructions for Her Majesty's Consuls (set out in full on page 37 of Fynn's *British Consuls Abroad*) that " Her Majesty's Commission and the exequatur will secure to the consul the enjoyment of such privileges, immunities, and exemptions as have been enjoyed generally by his predecessors, and as are usually granted to consuls in the country in which he resides; and he will be cautious not to aim at more."

*Greece:* "Consuls have not, as ambassadors and other public ministers, a representative character which places them under the law of nations. They are political agents, but only in this sense, that they are recognized by the sovereign who receives them as officers of the sovereign who sends them, and that their mandate has as a basis either positive treaties, common usage of nations, or the general public law." Instructions of 1834, Art. 2.

*Guatemala:* While there is no direct statement to the effect that consuls are not diplomatic agents, there is a necessary implication of that fact to be deduced from Paragraph 6 of the *Apéndice al Reglamento Diplomático y Consular de la República,* which also states that "Consuls necessarily 'have the right to certain privileges and exemptions' (not very well defined, and which vary according to treaties, customs, or permission of the country of residence) 'without which their charge would be very difficult.'"

*Honduras:* Honduras is one of the few states which have by law defined the extent of the immunities of foreign consuls functioning within the national boundaries. Article 1 of the *Ley sobre Misiones Consulares Extranjeras* is devoted to the consideration of the character of the consular office. "Honduras only recognizes in foreign consular missions the right to represent and protect the persons, interests, and property of their compatriots, within the limits of the jurisdiction in which they exercise their functions. In consequence, consular officers lack a diplomatic character; they are not representatives of the state which names them, nor can they consider themselves attached to that character." Nor is Honduras inconsistent in its position; for no higher standing is permitted to be claimed by Honduranean consuls, since Article 32 of the *Reglamento Consular* of 1906 is identical with Article 35 of the Chilean Regulations of 1897 *supra.*

*Mexico:* Mexico is another of the states which have passed

laws to clarify the situation relative to consular privileges. Unlike that of Honduras, the Mexican law does not contain a specific denial of the existence of the diplomatic character. However, the act goes into great detail in specifying just what exemptions foreign consuls may claim, and expressly denies the existence of any others. As the exemptions named, while comprehensive compared with those usually granted, are not so inclusive as those granted to diplomats, it is quite clear that the Government of Mexico does not consider the matter an open one—a conclusion which is reinforced by the fact that the law uses the term "commercial agent" as synonymous with consul throughout. *Ley para Fijar el Derecho Mexicano en Orden á Los Agentes Comerciales en el Territorio de la Nación* of 1859. The same is true of the *Reglamento de la Ley Orgánica del Servicio Consular Mexicano* of 1924 and of the *Ley Orgánica y Reglamento del Servicio Consular Mexicano* of 1911 which it superseded. Both of these applying to Mexican consuls abroad limit the claims of the Mexican consuls to such as they may base upon custom or reciprocity.

*Netherlands:* The British consul at Amsterdam on December 28, 1871, reported that the only privilege which consuls in that city enjoyed was exemption from all direct taxes. *Reports relative to British Consular Establishments*, Vol. II, p. 9.

*Peru:* The *Reglamento Consular del Peru* of 1897 carries in Article 28 a statement similar to that of the Argentine Regulations of 1862.

*Russia:* The Russian position seems to have passed from a denial of the existence of any other than a commercial character in a consul to that now assumed by the majority of states. Thus the *Reports relative to British Consular Establishments* (1872) contained among others, letters from the British consuls at various places in Russia, the general tenor of which is indicated by the extracts:

. . . no privileges attach to the position of consuls in this country. (Consul at St. Petersburg, February 3, 1872, vol. ii, p. 116.)

I enjoy no privileges by treaty or usage.

There are no privileges or jurisdiction enjoyed or exercised by my colleagues, any more than by myself. I know of no country where the position of consuls stands so low as in this part of Russia. We are treated simply as commercial agents —are refused any privilege but what is enjoyed by foreigners generally, and are scarcely recognized as public functionaries.

If we appeal for any alteration or improvement, we are accused of interfering with local regulations. (Consul at Kertch, Crimea, October 31, 1871, vol. ii, p. 89.)

The English consul general at Odessa possesses no privileges or jurisdiction beyond what is enjoyed by his consular colleagues, who by treaty come under the most-favored-nation clause. In fact, of privileges, I know of none now which a consul can claim more than a private individual of the same nation, excepting in one or two trifling matters, such as exemption from passport-tax whilst residing in the country, and the receipt of books for private use free of duty, and without being subject to the "censure." (Consul general at Odessa, 1871, vol. ii, p. 99.)

Consuls are held in little consideration, and have but slight influence here. (Consul at Taganrog, December 1, 1871, vol. ii, p. 126.)

A change was made in this position, however, before the fall of the Romanoffs. Baron Heyking in his work, *A Practical Guide for Russian Consular Officers,* lists a number of privileges which were enjoyed by foreign consuls in Russia at the time he wrote; and the Russian consul general at Seattle has in a letter commented upon the highly privileged position of such officers in his native state during the Empire. The unsettled conditions following the revolution were marked by a refusal of the Soviet Government to recognize the privileges usually accorded to consuls, according to the same letter, which, however, was written by a man with strong imperialist convictions. The legal position of foreign consuls under the new regime was defined in a decree issued in 1921. The London *Times* of July 19, 1921, carried a report to the effect that:

The *Isvestia* recently published a decree of the Soviet Government under which diplomatic immunities and extra-territoriality for representatives of foreign nations is reestablished. Consular officials will enjoy the usual privileges.

A despatch from the American consul at Viborg, Finland, to the Secretary of State, under date of July 28, 1921, contains a summary of a decree (of July 7, 1921), presumably the one mentioned in the *Times* despatch, on the position of consular representatives in Russia. This summary contains a list of privileges, more restricted than those of diplomatic officers, which definitely aligns the Soviet Government with the leading states of the world in this respect.

*Salvador:* The Salvadorean *Ley sobre Misiones Consulares Extranjeras* which defines the position of foreign consuls in that state contains in Article 1 a provision identical with that of the Honduranean law of the same name. Article 40 of that law denies to consuls any claim to the privilege of extraterritoriality.

*Uruguay:* "Consular agents in a foreign country are under the special protection of international law, but they should not claim the immunities and privileges which belong solely to diplomatic agents" according to Article 40 of the *Reglamento por el cual Deben Regirse los Cónsules de la República Oriental del Uruguay en el Ejercicio de sus Funciones* bearing the date of 1878. Such is a correct statement of the Uruguayan position today, though the Regulations of 1906 (Art. 71) and of 1917 (Art. 56) use language similar to that of Article 112 of the Chilean Regulations of 1915, *supra.*

*Venezuela:* By decree of June 27, 1912, it has been established that "Consuls, vice consuls, and other employees of this category, whatever be the name by which they are designated, will be considered in Venezuela as commercial agents, without diplomatic character, and as such will not enjoy other immunities than those accorded in the decree of January 25, 1883 . . ." *Gaceta Oficial,* June 28, 1912. The decree is also published in Chile's *Boletín de Relaciones Esteriores,* 1914, vol. I, no. 42, p. 3. The relevant part of the decree of January 25, 1883, issued by President Guzman Blanco, was taken from a report of Vice President A. L. Guzman under date of April 12, 1852, and reads as follows:

> . . . the Government . . . as a point of positive public law has decided that consuls . . . do not enjoy personal immunities, exemptions, or privileges, which lessen in any manner the territorial jurisdiction, whether they be or have been named by the Government of the Republic in foreign ports, or be or have been named by friendly governments for the ports and cities of the Republic; that this does not diminish the independence to which the Government recognizes they have the right in order to exercise the functions of their charge, when they are in accord with the laws in force in the territory in which they are acting. (Contained in Seijas, *El Derecho Internacional Hispano-Americano,* vol. i, p. 432.)

This position has been reinforced by the passage of a law declaring functions of consuls and diplomatic agents to be incompatible and refusing to permit any person to be accredited to Venezuela in both capacities. The statute was upheld when Peru appointed a consul general and chargé d'affaires; after an exchange of notes the individual appointed was recognized as chargé but without any consular duties. See Venezuelan *Libro Amarillo* for 1923, pp. 252 and 253.

*Other states:* In addition to the above list of states which have clearly committed themselves to the position that consuls are not diplomatic agents but nevertheless enjoy some privileges, may be added others whose official pronouncements do not treat of the matter directly, but none the less assume that as the basis of the provisions which are made. Among these are Brazil (*Consular Regulations* of 1830), Dominican Republic (*Ley Orgánica del Cuerpo Consular de la República Dominicana,* 1877), Ecuador (*Reglamento Consular,* 1870), Nicaragua (*Reglamento Consular,* 1880), and Paraguay (*Reglamento Consular,* 1871).

*United States:* The first stand taken by the United States was a clear denial of any diplomatic character of consuls and of any protection of the law of nations for these officers; but over a period of years, marked by a series of diplomatic communications, opinions of attorneys general, and departmental regulations, that position has been changed in part; and it may be said that since 1854 the United States has uniformly maintained that consuls are entitled to some privileges under international law. This development is shown in the accompanying extracts, the first from a statement by Jefferson as Secretary for Foreign Affairs:

The law of nations does not of itself extend to consuls at all. They are not of the diplomatic class of characters to which alone that law extends of right. Convention indeed may give it to them, and sometimes has done so; but in that case the convention can be produced. . . . Independently of (a special) law, consuls are to be considered as distinguished foreigners, dignified by a commission from their sovereign, and specially recommended by him to the respect of the Nation with whom they reside. They are subject to the laws of the land indeed precisely as other foreigners are, a convention where there is one making a part of the laws of the land; but, if at any time, their conduct should render it necessary to assert the authority of the laws over them, the rigor of these laws should be tempered by our respect for their sovereign, as far as the case will admit. This moderate and respectful treatment towards foreign consuls it is my duty to recommend, and press upon our citizens, because I ask it for their good, towards our own consuls, from the people with whom they reside. (Jefferson, Sec. for For. Affs., to Mr. Newton, Sept. 8, 1791; Moore, *Digest of International Law,* V: p. 33.)

Two years later Mr. Jefferson as Secretary of State was the author of another communication to the same effect. See Moore, *Digest,* V: 34.

The same position was at least inferentially maintained by the Attorney General on November 21, 1797. Asked for his opinion on a consul's privilege from legal process, Attorney General Lee interpreted the French convention of 1788 in this manner:

> The second article of the convention seems to me to preclude all doubt respecting the suability of the consul-general. The immunities and privileges annexed to his office are therein distinctly enumerated; and in all other respects, he is subject to the laws as our own citizens are. (I Ops. 45.)

While this language might be interpreted to mean that a consul under the general rules of international law would have those immunities specified in the treaty, it is unlikely that the framers of the treaty would incorporate just those immunities already existing under international law; and it is not probable that the Attorney General would have interpreted the immunities of consuls so differently from the Department of State without giving his reason therefor. Moreover, the problem of the consul's position in the absence of treaty was not before the Attorney General. In any event, the opinion was never taken to imply that consuls had any exemptions under the law of nations; on the contrary, it has been cited to show that no such immunities existed. See *Consular Regulations,* 1856, p. 20.

As Secretary of State, Monroe apparently continued in the view held by his predecessor; for, in his estimation, while consuls were undoubtedly entitled to great respect as bearing the commissions of their sovereign, "their duties are of a commercial nature and their public character subaltern; neither their persons nor their domicile have heretofore been protected as have those of ambassadors and other public ministers." (Monroe, Sec. of State, to Mr. Harris, Chargé at St. Petersburg, July 31, 1816; Moore *Digest,* V: 67.)

Three years later when Adams was Secretary of State, there was a prima facie departure from this consistent denial as is shown in his statement that:

> Consuls are indeed received by the government from acknowledged sovereign powers with whom they have no treaty. But the exequatur for a consul-general can obviously not be granted without recognizing the authority from whom his appointment proceeds as sovereign. "The consul," says Vattel (book 2, chap. 2, sec. 34), "is not a public minister; *but as he is charged with a commission from his sovereign,* and received in that quality by them where he resides, he should enjoy, to a certain extent, the protection of the law of nations." (Adams, Sec. of State, to the President, Jan. 28, 1819; Moore, *Digest,* V: 13.)

Vattel took the fact that a consul received a commission from his sovereign, as a basis upon which he might establish consular immunities. Adams was interested in Vattel's premise, not his conclusion; and the fact that he cited Vattel as an authority that reception of a consul would involve recognition of his sovereign, did not necessarily commit him to Vattel's corollary. It is probable that the portion of Vattel dealing with immunities was quoted merely to complete the sentence; and this view is strengthened by the fact that it was extraneous to Adams's purpose and that the succeeding sentence in which Vattel developed his statement was not quoted. If this be the correct interpretation, the contradiction is apparent rather than real.

Wirt, as Attorney General, was called upon, December 1, 1820, to render an opinion in a case in which the Spanish vice-consul at New Orleans claimed to be exempt from arrest in a civil suit. In deciding that the consul was subject to the civil jurisdiction of American courts (which was the only question involved) the Attorney General stated generally that consuls were not entitled to the protection of the law of nations. (I Ops. 300.)

Again in 1830 the existence of consular immunities on an international law basis was denied, this time by Van Buren, as Secretary of State. (Circular, May 5, 1830; Moore, *Digest,* V : 34.) But the clearest official denial came on September 26, 1835 in an opinion by Attorney General Butler in response to a direct request by the Secretary of State for his opinion on the immunities of foreign consuls. In the opinion, the Attorney General stated that:

After a careful consideration of this subject, I am of opinion that foreign consuls in the United States are entitled to no immunities beyond those enjoyed by persons coming to this country in a private capacity from foreign nations, except that of being sued and prosecuted exclusively in the United States courts, under the jurisdiction conferred on them by the Constitution and laws of the United States. The question whether consuls are entitled to the privileges belonging to public ministers, has been much discussed by writers on the law of nations and in the English and American courts of justice. The statements of Chancellor Kent in his recent *Commentaries on American Law* (vol. i, sec. 2) are fully supported by the textbooks and decisions to which he refers; and I therefore take the liberty of quoting them, as expressing my own opinion on this point. (I Ops. 1005.)

The opinion of Chancellor Kent to which the Attorney General referred purports to give the law as it was "settled" at the time of publication, not as the author thought it should be. In the light of the Attorney General's comment the following extract from Kent's *Commentaries* takes on an official aspect:

A consul is not such a public minister as to be entitled to the privileges appertaining to that character, nor is he under the special protection of the law of nations. He is entitled to privileges to a certain extent, such as for safe conduct, but he is not entitled to the *jus gentium*. Vattel thinks that his functions require that he should be independent of the ordinary criminal jurisdiction of the country, and that he ought to be sent home to be punished. But no such immunities have been conferred on consuls by the modern practice of nations, and it may be considered as settled law, that consuls do not enjoy the protection of the law of nations, any more than any other persons who enter the country under a safe-conduct. In civil and criminal cases they are equally subject to the laws of the country in which they reside. The same doctrine, declared by public jurists, has been frequently laid down in the English and American courts of justice.

Not long after the opinion of Attorney General Butler denying consuls the protection of the law of nations, the United States began to recede from that position and to develop the one maintained today—a step which was almost a necessity for a progressive commercial nation with consuls all over the globe. Slightly more than one year after Attorney General Butler had emphatically held that "foreign consuls in the United States are entitled to no immunities," Secretary of State Forsyth referred to the imprisonment of an American consul in France as "an infraction of the law of nations." The extent of this innovation may be seen from the following quotation:

It is believed that under the laws and usages of France favors and exemptions are extended to foreign consuls, and that in conducting his defense Mr. Croxall's proper course (in a proceeding against him for assault) would have been to plead the privileges of his official character. However this may be, the imprisonment of an American consul residing in a foreign port is a serious evil and inconvenience, not only as lessening his influence as an officer of his government, but as calculated to produce, in some cases, injurious effects on the interests of American citizens confided to him, and to reflect dishonor on his country. Vattel says (vol. ii, chap. ii, sec. 34) that a sovereign "by the very act of receiving a consul, tacitly engages to allow him all the liberty and safety necessary in the proper discharge of his functions, without which the admission of the consul would be insignificant and deceptive." And, again, speaking of consular functions, the same author observes that "they seem to require that the consul should be independent of the *ordinary criminal justice* of the place where he resides, so as not to be molested or imprisoned, unless he himself violates the law of nations by some enormous misdemeanor." Our Constitution recognizes this doctrine by providing that in all cases affecting consuls the Supreme Court alone shall have original jurisdiction. (Forsyth, Sec. of State, to Mr. Cass, Dec. 6, 1836; Moore, *Digest*, V: 68.)

Forsyth is a far cry from Jefferson. Reciprocity, urged by the latter, as a basis for the proper treatment of consuls is displaced by an appeal to the laws and usages of France with a discreet silence about the laws and customs of the United States. Mr. Forsyth was hard put for a shadow of a claim to reciprocity when he was forced to call to his assistance the provisions of the Constitution. The chief significance of the statement is that the United States was unwilling to have the same rule applied to its consuls that was being applied to foreign consuls in the United States, an attitude which ultimately led to a change in the American practice.

Less than two years later, in another note on this same case, Secretary Forsyth modified his position in a marked degree when he stated that if Mr. Croxall

stood upon the same ground as all other foreign consuls whose governments had not entered into conventional stipulations with France to secure to those functionaries certain privileges and immunities, the United States have no special reason to complain of the course of proceeding against him. It nevertheless appeared to the President that the imprisonment of Mr. Croxall while holding his commission from the United States, and his exequatur from the French government, was not called for by the occasion, and that any restraint upon him, rendering impracticable the performance of his consular duties, if consonant to national law, was not consistent with national comity, as exercised in France to other friendly powers. (Forsyth, Sec. of State, to Mr. Cass, April 13, 1838; Moore, *Digest,* V: 68.)

That his position was not to be construed as maintaining that a consul was entitled to diplomatic immunities was shown by a statement of Secretary Forsyth in 1839, in which he reiterated the position that a consul was not a public minister and, even in the absence of an accredited minister, could not lay claim to the privileges usually accorded diplomatic functionaries. Forsyth, Sec. of State, to Mr. Hagerdon, Sept. 7, 1839; Moore, *Digest,* V: 36.

The net result of the correspondence of Secretary Forsyth seems to be the abandonment of the position that the consul is not under the protection of the law of nations, and the substitution for it of certain, as yet undefined, privileges (among which under some circumstances at least might be included exemption from imprisonment on a criminal charge) under that law. Yet in 1849 Secretary of State Clayton expressed his opinion that a consul was liable to be punished to the same extent as other foreign residents for a criminal violation of the local law of the country of his residence

(Clayton, Sec. of State, to Mr. Calderon de la Barca, Aug. 28, 1849; Moore, *Digest,* V: 34); and it is clear that such a violation of the law in many cases would be followed by arrest and imprisonment as a part of the punishment.

The situation was approached from an entirely different angle when President Fillmore in his message of 1851 informed Congress of the riots in the City of New Orleans which resulted in the subjection of the Spanish vice consul to insults and in loss of property to the consulate. The problem presented was not that of exempting consular officers from certain obligations, but of protecting them in the exercise of their functions. In presenting the matter to Congress, the President again reverted to reciprocity, as the following extract from his second annual message will show:

> Ministers and consuls of foreign nations are the means and agents of communication between us and those nations, and it is of the utmost importance that while residing in the country they should feel a perfect security so long as they faithfully discharge their respective duties and are guilty of no violation of our laws. This is the admitted law of nations. . . . And what is due to our own public functionaries residing in foreign nations is exactly the measure of what is due to the functionaries of other Governments residing here. As in war the bearers of flags of truce are sacred, or else wars would be interminable, so in peace ambassadors, public ministers and consuls charged with friendly national intercourse are objects of especial respect and protection, each according to the rights belonging to his rank and station. (Richardson, *Messages and Papers of the Presidents,* V: 118.)

According to the President's view the office of consul has inherent in it a certain claim to protection by the receiving nation, a protection which must be accorded if the consular office is to fulfill its mission, and which has been accorded by the law of nations. Here again reciprocity was given as a reason for consular privileges; but while Jefferson cited only reciprocity, Fillmore cited a law of nations in which reciprocity determined not the fact of protection but only the amount to be extended in a particular case.

In conducting the correspondence arising from this incident, Secretary of State Webster made a clear distinction between the protection due a foreign consul accredited in the United States and that due to foreigners residing here merely as private individuals engaged in trade and commerce. (Webster, Sec. of State, to Mr. Calderon de la Barca, November 13, 1851; Wharton, *Digest,* Vol. II, p. 60.) This indicated a considerable advance over Butler's statement that a consul was on the same plane with any other foreigner who entered the country, and seems to be in complete accord with the President's views of the consular office.

The opinions of Attorney General Cushing in 1854 and 1855 were marked by a definiteness for the first time shown in an American treatment of the subject; and they indicate that American opinion had at last turned definitely in favor of consular immunities. From this time the point in issue was not the existence of consular immunities but their extent. The first of these opinions was on the right of consuls to celebrate marriages. While the Attorney General denied that consuls were public ministers entitled to the immunities of diplomatic agents, he stated:

> In truth, all the obscurity and contradiction as to this point in different authors arise from the fact that consuls do unquestionably enjoy certain privileges of exemption from local and political obligation; but still these privileges are limited, and fall very far short of the right of exterritoriality. (VII Ops. 18.)

Without discussing the extent of the immunities which the Attorney General recognized as existing, it is worthy of note that he was of the opinion that consuls " do unquestionably" enjoy certain exemptions. From this time on the United States has been aligned with the third group mentioned above, and has definitely recognized that while consuls are not public ministers, they are entitled to some exemptions, though the extent of these has varied from time to time.

Pertinent parts of the *Consular Regulations* of 1856 are molded along the lines laid down in the opinions of Attorney General Cushing. Thus we find that "consuls possess, moreover, by the law of nations many functions, rights, and privileges, other than such as are defined by convention, by legislative act, or by regulation." (Page 13.) And further, "His commission and exequatur will enable him to exercise and enjoy all the rights, exemptions, privileges, and powers to the same appertaining, and such as are usually granted to consuls in the country in which the consulate is situated; and he will seek for none greater without authority from the Department of State." (Page 40.) The Regulations also contain the extract from Cushing's opinion set out above.

On the other hand, the Regulations state (p. 20) that "A consul is not such a public minister as to be entitled to the privileges appertaining to that character, nor is he under the special protection of the law of nations." To the first part of the sentence, no exception can be taken; but the second part is in direct conflict with the view of President Fillmore set out above, and seems to be contrary to the earlier statement in the same volume that "consuls possess, moreover, by the law of nations many functions, rights, and privileges." When it is taken into consideration that among the authorities for the denial of the protection of the law of nations is Kent, it becomes apparent that the inconsistency is a real one. The explanation probably is that the Regulations were compiled without any special thought being given to the subject of consular privileges, and consequently no consideration was given to the change in American position since Kent wrote. At best the most compelling authority for Kent's statement is the fact that it was adopted by Attorney General Butler; against it we have the statement of Attorney General Cushing. The authority for the two being equal, the later in time will naturally prevail, and the recognition of the existence of certain privileges on an international law basis must stand. The inconsistency of statement regarding this matter, unfortunately, is not novel; witness, for instance, the lament voiced by Mr. Cushing in 1856 in one of his opinions:

> No well-established universality of international rule exists on the subject of the immunities of consuls accredited between the states of Christendom. Of course, there is a diversity of practical administration on this point, according to the tenor of the treaties, the customary law, the legislative enactments, and the executive regulations of each particular country. And the incompleteness of provision, and the uncertainty of doctrine, are especially notable in Great Britain and the United States. (VIII Ops. 169.)

But if any doubt remained as to the relative correctness of these two conflicting statements, it was resolved by the revision of the *Consular Regulations* which appeared in 1881, where in the midst of a lengthy statement of consular privileges appears the following:

> Although consuls have no right to claim the privileges and immunities of diplomatic representatives, they are under the special protection of international law, and are regarded as the officers both of the state which appoints them and state which receives them.

The latest bound edition of the *Consular Regulations,* that issued in 1896, repeats the provision of the edition of 1881; and the loose-leaf revision issued in 1923 makes no changes in this regard, so that today the United States definitely recognizes that under international law a consul may claim a certain protection and certain privileges, while he may not pretend to the immunities of a diplomatic officer.

# CHAPTER II

## Inviolability of Consular Archives

Inviolability of the consular archives is almost universally considered as essential to the discharge of the consular office. The question of what constitutes the archives does not present much difficulty; consular regulations frequently go into considerable detail in the specification of the exact titles of the records which are included in that category. Generally, it may be said that all official papers, records and documents in the possession of the consul in the discharge of his duties form a part of the archives. More specifically, the following are clearly stamped with this character: communications between the consul and his government; correspondence on official matters with the diplomatic and other consular officers of his government; communications with the central (where permitted) and the local authorities of the receiving state; correspondence with the officers of third states when on official matters; correspondence with private individuals in furtherance of the consular functions; information acquired and put on record by the consul in the discharge of his duties; and the various books and records which his government requires him to keep. The distinguishing characteristic of this group of papers is that all have come into the possession of the consul by virtue of his consular office, as distinguished from his position as a private individual.

The protection which international law extends applies only to these official documents; any attempt on the part of the consular officer to secure protection for private papers is an abuse of his position. Because of this fact it is the usual practice of governments to require their consuls to keep the official records separate from private files. Consuls are commanded to provide, wherever practicable to do so, a separate apartment for the archives; and this apartment is to be the one designated by the coat of arms. Where a separate apartment is not feasible, consuls are instructed frequently to use a separate cabinet, case, or at least a shelf, which in case of necessity can be shut off from the rest of the room and sealed. This distinction is fundamentally sound: in the case of consuls engaged in private business, it is imperative; and in no case is there any reason to place the consul with respect to his private correspondence on a different plane from that occupied by other foreigners in the country.

Inevitably the question will arise at times as to the classification of a particular paper. Of this, the better rule would seem to be that the consul is the judge in the first instance; otherwise it would be possible for the local authorities to limit unduly the extent of privilege conferred under international law. True, an appeal to the central authorities from the action of the local officers might result in a substantiation of the claim of the consul and a restoration of the document in question; but the damage would have been done—the consul would have been deprived of the paper in the interim and the contents of the paper would have been made known. Obviously such a power of determination might be abused by the consul as well as by the local authorities. In such an event, however, the state of residence would not be without recourse, for a note to the government which had appointed the consul would result in an examination of the question by a state department which would have no incentive to interfere in the private affairs of its consuls, or to shield its officers in an evasion of local law. The delay which would be incident to such a procedure is preferable to the irremediable exposure which would follow the other rule. Furthermore, if the receiving state believes that a consul is abusing his privilege in this respect, it always has available a request for his recall or the more drastic measure of revocation of the exequatur.

Though it is true that the problem of determining who is to judge the official character of a paper may be open to question, there can certainly be no defense of a consul's action in depositing a purely private paper in the archives, or of accepting a paper from any other person and placing it among the archives to share the protection of the latter. Even in such an extreme instance, however, it is believed that the proper course of the offended government is to appeal to the consul's government for a disavowal of the actions of its officer and for instructions to him to comply with the demands of the receiving government. This was the procedure followed in an analogous case under the Franco-American consular convention of 1853. In that treaty, provision was made for the inviolability of the consular offices, which resulted in the protection of all objects within those offices. The American consul at Nice permitted a private individual to deposit property in the consular offices in order to escape attachment in pursuance of legal proceedings. Upon request of the French government that of the United States promptly disavowed the action of its consul and instructed him to return the property to its owner, giving the French authorities notice as to the time at which the delivery was to be made. The procedure followed by both governments was eminently correct, and probably would be followed in the case of an irregular deposit in the consular archives.

Conceding the official nature of the papers in the archives, it seems that the consul may claim the protection of international law as a right. Nearly all governments speak of the archives as inviolable, and that without reference to any local custom. It is to be noted that the various consular regulations directing a claim of inviolability are issued to control the actions of national consuls on foreign soil, so that recognition of inviolability is not a matter of municipal law. If an almost universal statement to consuls to require inviolability of the consular archives, coupled with an equally extensive granting of such inviolability can serve to create or to recognize a right in international law, then inviolability of consular archives can be claimed a matter of right today.

In its nature the exemption of the consular archives from the control of the local authorities is one which inheres in the consular office and is independent of the person of the consul. The immunity is that of the government, not of the consular officer; and in consequence it may be waived only by the government. A consul's act in opening the archives to the examination of outsiders would lay him open to censure by his superiors. As the right is one which may not be waived by the consul, it would seem that the government which has received him should never call upon him to give its officers access to any part of the consular records, addressing its request to the persons who have the right to grant such permission. Nor, of course, is such a request lightly to be made.

What can not be accomplished directly by opening the archives to persons not authorized by the consul's government to examine them, can not be accomplished indirectly by compelling the consul to testify before a court as to their contents. In cases where consuls are properly before local courts, either as defendants or as witnesses, their testimony must be confined to those facts of which they are in possession in an individual capacity, and may not include those of which they are possessed by virtue of their office. This rule applies whether a subpoena *duces tecum* has issued to compel the consul to produce the books of the consulate or whether the attempt is merely to secure such information as as the consul may be able to recall.[1]

So great is the respect to which the archives are entitled that whenever any action of the receiving government, such for instance as the arrest and imprisonment of the consul, must result in the consul's being unable to be present to see that the inviolability of the archives is respected, time and opportunity should be granted him for placing these documents under the consular seal to insure their sanctity in his absence. This is the logical result of the principle of inviolability; it is expressly recognized in the municipal laws of some states and, it is believed, in the practice of others.

The extent of the immunity is indicated by the terms selected to express it in the various official documents dealing with the subject. A perusal of these shows that the local authorities under no "claim", "pretext", or "motive" can "search", "seize", "attach", "examine", "investigate", "sequestrate", or "damage" the archives. The evident intention of the framers of the regulations is to cover every conceivable claim that can be put forward as the basis of a demand for access to the records. Consuls are sometimes stated to be "responsible" for the archives under the above conditions; while municipal laws in some states threaten drastic punishment for the individual who seeks to do any of the forbidden acts.

That the archives are the property of the government, not the personal property of the consul, would hardly seem open to question; but consular regulations at times carry a definite statement to that effect. Such being the case it is inconceivable that any court would permit the attachment or seizure

[1] *Infra*, p. 138.

of the archives as security for the payment of a debt incurred by a consul in his private capacity. However, this is what William Beach Lawrence states was done at Manchester, England in the case of a suit brought against the American consul to compel the payment of his debts.[1] Hall places the incident in the realm of fiction;[2] but an independent investigation shows that the records of the Department of State support Lawrence. The consular regulations of a few states make specific provision on this point by asserting that the archives and property of the consulate may never be alienated, nor constituted or considered a pledge or guaranty without the consent of the government.

A somewhat closer case occurs in the possible attempt to seize the archives as security for the payment of rates or taxes levied against the building occupied by the consular office. There all questions of a personal nature are eliminated; the problem is simply whether official government property, the archives may be used to insure the payment of an obligation contracted by the agent on behalf of his government and clearly within the scope of his authority. Though the London incident cited by Calvo[3] is contra, it seems that even in this case the inviolability of the archives should be respected. The mutual importance of the con-

[1] In 1858 "the consular property at Manchester, belonging to the United States—flag, seal, arms, record-books, etc.—were levied on by the sheriff for a private debt of the consul, and were not released till security had been given by a private citizen in the absence of the consul. Mr. Dallas, Minister in London, was instructed to pay the bill and thus save from sale the consular archives. Department of State MS." Lawrence, second edition of Wheaton, p. 427, Lawrence's note number 143. An account of the incident is given by Lawrence in *RDI*, X: 317.

[2] Hall, *International Law*, third and later editions, note to section 105.

[3] M. Clunet investigated the alleged incident reported in Calvo's *Le Droit International*, section 1395; and on the authority of the British Foreign Office and Inland Revenue Office "relegated this story to the domain of fiction." *JDIP*, 1888, p. 66.

sular system to the states concerned, and the fact that the archives are indispensable to the conduct of the consular office; the further fact that the intrinsic value of the consular archives is practically nil, their value being derived from their contents and being incapable of being realized upon unless those contents are known—one of the contingencies sought to be guarded against by the concession of inviolability—all argue for the records being left in the possession of the consular officer. And to this reasoning must be added the authority of a large number of cases holding that even a suit *in rem* against property admitted to be government owned is an action against the government, which can not be brought without the consent of the government. The resulting suspension of consular activities could have a justification only if there were no other way of collecting the amount due; and it is inconceivable that such could ever be the case. In both types of cases considered the question is fundamentally between the consul and his government, whether the interests of the latter can be best served by one whose actions lead to such difficulties; and when the facts are brought to the attention of the sending government, the desired result will be reached without any of the inconveniences of direct action.

Another question which may at times become important is the extent to which the immunity conferred on the archives extends to the locality in which they are situated. In some cases this is involved with a claim of inviolability for the entire consular office; in another form it has given rise to a claim of inviolability for those fixtures which because of their intimate connection with the archives might seem to have been invested with some of their privileged character. No record has been found of any attempt on the part of a government to determine this point in the absence of a treaty provision. Clearly there must be some depository for the consular records; and equally clearly a seizure of the depository might afford the seizing parties an opportunity to take cognizance of the contents, and might interrupt the consular business. In view of these facts, it would seem desirable that such fixtures as are necessary for the proper safekeeping of the consular archives should share the inviolability of their contents. This much seems essential; beyond it the only safe reliance is a treaty provision.[1]

The above considerations apply in times of peace; in time of war the place of the archives is much less certain. The usual procedure is for the archives to be left in the care of the consul of a neutral state; it would seem that they should then enjoy the protection which would be afforded the archives of that consulate. But whatever may be the theory, it seems that consular archives were violated during the World War.[2]

The following statements are typical of the position assumed by states today on the point of inviolability of the consular archives:

*Argentina:* Under article 363 of the regulations of 1906:

> The consular archives, as well as the seals, coats of arms, flags, and other furniture and fixtures which figure in the inventory of the office, or which have been acquired since the taking of the inventory, are the inviolable property of the nation.

[1] As a result of the so-called "Florence incident" in which Italian officials acting under order of an Italian court entered the French consulate at Florence and seized a part of the records in connection with a suit in a local court, the two states involved entered into a treaty to prevent such action in the future. In that compact the term "consular archives" was defined to apply to the parts of the chancellery dedicated to the deposit of the records as well as to the documents themselves. For an account of the incident and a discussion of the points involved, see *JDIP* (1888), XV, 53 *et seq.*

[2] See Portugal and Turkey, *infra*, pp. 49 and 50; also Garner, *International Law and the World War*, I: 47-53 on the treatment of the persons of consuls as well as of the archives; and *JDI*, 43: 527 *et seq.*

And under article 364 the papers constituting the archives are to be kept separate from the private books and papers of the consular officer, a distinct place which can be shut off to itself when necessary to be utilized if possible.

In 1919 the legation and consulates of Austria within the Argentine Republic were closed. As the archives were to remain within Argentine territory, the Austrian minister at Buenos Aires requested that their inviolability be recognized; and in November of that year the inviolability was conceded. *Memoria del Ministerio de Relaciones Esteriores,* 1919-1921, p. 41.

*Bolivia:* Article 11 of the regulations of 1877 authorizes consuls to claim prerogatives and exemptions which are generally conceded by the custom of the place where they are located, and adds, " They will claim as essential to the exercise of their charge, the inviolability of their archives and papers, and the independence of their acts appropriate to their consular character." A statement to the same effect was incorporated into article 21 of the regulations of 1887, while article 76 of that compilation requires the separation of official from private papers, the official papers being the property of the nation (article 77).

In title seven of the same document under the heading " Foreign Consuls Resident in Bolivia " article 98 carries the short blanket statement: " Archives and papers of the consulate are inviolable ".

*Brazil:*

The archives, documents, and official correspondence of foreign consulates and vice consulates are exempt from search, and from all or any kind of investigation or examination on the part of the authorities of the empire. In case of the imprisonment or expulsion of a consular agent, without the presence of some person to take his place, the said archives, documents, and correspondence are to be carefully preserved, being sealed with wax by the said agent and by the chief judicial authority residing in the district. (Article XIX of the imperial decree of 1851, contained in *British State Papers*, vol. 42, p. 1316.)

In 1871 the British consul at Rio de Janeiro reported the recognition of the inviolability of the consular archives. *Reports relative to British Consular Establishments,* Vol. IV: 143.

*Chile:* Consuls must claim the inviolability of their archives as essential to the discharge of their functions, according to article 17 of the regulations of 1860. In 1897 the article was changed to read:

Article 189. The consular archives are the inviolable property of the nation, as are also the seals, coats of arms, flags and all the furniture which compose the inventory which each consul must make to take possession of his charge and to transmit it to his successor, and they can not be alienated, or constituted or considered a pledge or guarantee of responsibility.

In 1915 the separation of private from official papers was commanded (article 323) and the immunity of the latter was expressed (article 113) as " . . . their archives and papers are inviolable and it will never be permitted that these be touched by outside authorities under any pretext ".

*Colombia:* The consular archives must be kept separate from the private property of the consul; and the former are the " inviolable property of the nation ". *Guiá Consular de la República,* pages 25 and 69; and article 67 of the law of 1866. To the same effect is the *Manual Consular Colombiano* of Perez-Sarmiento, page 30.

*Costa Rica:* Article 215 of the regulations of 1888 provided for the isolation of the consular archives, and article 214 spoke of them as the property of the nation, while article 27 instructed consuls to claim as essential to the exercise of their consular functions the inviolability of their archives and papers. This was continued in the *Ley Orgánica del Servicio Consular* of 1920 by a provision that:

> In no case, under no claim or pretext, shall consuls confide the papers pertaining to their archives to foreign persons or authorities, reserving them at all times under the strictest responsibility. (Article 75.)

The separation of the official documents from private papers was likewise provided for in this edition, article 95.

*Cuba:* Archives are the property of the state (page 13) left in charge of consuls, who " in every case must maintain the inviolability of the consular archives " (pages 6, 7). *Instrucciones Provisionales para el Servicio Consular.*

*Denmark:* " It being a rule of international law that consular archives are inviolable and that they must not under any circumstances be searched through or seized by the local authorities, it is of importance to keep them separate from, and never to mix them with, other papers." Paragraphs 46 and 79 of *Instructions pour les Consuls de Danemark á l'Étranger.*

*Dominican Republic:* The *Ley Orgánica del Cuerpo Consular de la República Dominicana* in articles 10 and 18 states that the archives are the property of the nation and are inviolable.

*Ecuador:* Inviolability of consular archives is essential to the exercise of consular functions. *Reglamento Consular,* 1870, article 17.

*Esthonia:* " Consular archives are inviolable to full extent " according to a translation of a newspaper article containing instructions issued by the Chief Police Administration forwarded by the legation at Riga, Latvia, to the Department of State under date of Dec. 7, 1922.

*France:* The *Répertoire des Pandectes Françaises* contains a digest of official and unofficial statements and decisions regarding various consular privileges; and those cited under numbers 97, 100 and 101 (vol. 21, pp. 379, 380) fully support the assertion that the inviolability of the consular archives is complete.

Inviolability of the archives was likewise reported by the British consul at Havre on Dec. 1, 1871. *Reports relative to British Consular Establishments,* vol. I, page 124.

*Great Britain:* This country is frequently pointed out as the one great exception to the rule that all states recognize the inviolability of consular archives. Such a statement is found in the works of a large number of English, French, and Spanish writers. It is believed that the assertion rests upon two incidents: one a sale of French archives at auction in London, reported by Calvo; and the other a seizure of the American archives at Manchester as security for the payment of a private debt of the consul. This last incident was reported by William Beach Lawrence. Of the two, that reported by Calvo has been most widely circulated and most frequently cited as authority, especially in Latin America. M. Clunet's investigations of this alleged incident led to his relegating it to the domain of fiction. Thus the entire burden of constituting England an exception must rest upon a single incident which occurred in 1858. Allué Salvador in his work *La Condición Jurídica de los Cónsules* points out that the celebrity of the London and Manchester incidents is proof of their rarity; [1] and he might have added that it is unfair in the extreme to place England in opposition to the rest of the world on the strength of a single incident occurring nearly three-quarters of a century ago when there has been daily opportunity, and perhaps some occasion, for the violation of the archives since that time. [2]

What is thought to be the real English rule is to be

[1] Page 93.

[2] For a fuller consideration of these incidents see *supra,* p. 40.

found in a note from the acting secretary to the Governor of Bombay to the American consul at Bombay on April 4, 1919:

As regards your statement that you are instructed to claim inviolability for the archives and official property of your office, I am directed to state that the Government of Bombay recognize the inviolability of such consular documents, and are informing the Court of Small Causes that it is inadvisable that their production should be enforced.

*Greece:* " In any case it is not permitted the local authorities to seize the correspondence of the office of a consul." Instructions, 1834, art. 3, par. 7.

*Haiti:* Under the law of 1912 the exemption of consular archives from searches and seizures is made to depend upon reciprocity. Art. 27. The archives must be kept separate from other papers.

*Honduras:* The law on foreign consuls expressly recognizes an absolute inviolability of archives in these terms:

Article 35. The consular office will be established in a special place excluded from other uses, even though the consuls be merchant or honorary, placing over the door an inscription which expresses its character. Books, papers, and other things pertaining to the consular office will be kept there. The archives and papers will be inviolably respected and on no motive or pretext can the authorities attach or take cognizance of them.

Article 39. The official acts of consuls and the correspondence with their Government, with the diplomatic agent of their country, or with any other consuls or authorities, are under the protection of international law and may not be the object of investigation on the part of the authorities of the State.

*Liberia:* " Their archives are inviolable and under no pretext will they permit them to be touched by any foreign authority whatever." Consular Regulations, article 28.

*Mexico:* The law of 1859 after stating that the offices of foreign consuls in Mexico shall be used for no other purposes, continues:

There will be kept here all the books, papers, and other things which pertain to the consular office. The archives and papers shall be respected as inviolate, and under no motive or pretext can the authorities seize or take cognizance of them. (Article 27.)

The law further provides that when the consul is to be imprisoned for any cause, sufficient time must be given him in which to place the archives under seal. During this operation, the arresting officer may not in any manner take cognizance of the contents of the archives, confining his efforts to such assistance as the consul may request of him. Article 28.

The provision for foreign consuls made in article 27 is quite similar to the one claimed for Mexican consular officers. See Consular Regulations of 1871, art. 98. This was restated in the regulations of 1911 as "Only with the authorization of the Secretary of Foreign Relations can they show to the authorities who seek them, the documents of their archives, inviolable in their nature." The entire subject of consular privileges was re-arranged in the consular regulations of 1923, where consular immunities were grouped according to whether their basis was international law or treaty or local custom. Among those which the consul was instructed to claim under international law is inviolability of archives. Article 53.

*Netherlands:* No mention is made of inviolability of archives in the *Netherlands' Consular Service Rules and Regulations,* 1908, paragraph 7 of which requires that the archives be kept separate from personal documents.

*Nicaragua:* Like the Netherlands, Nicaragua in the regulations of 1880, article 114, provided for the separation of official and personal documents without any statement as to inviolability.

*Peru:* Consular archives must not be mixed with the personal papers of the consular officer (regulations, 1897, art. 202; 1888, art. 223; 1863, art. 119); and being the inviolable property of the nation, they may not be pledged (1897, art. 203; 1888, art. 224; and see 1863, art. 120).

*Portugal:* One of the incidents set out in the German note of March 9, 1916 declaring war on Portugal was that " the archives of the imperial vice consul at Mossamedes were seized ". *International Law Situations,* 1917, page 105.

*Russia:* Under the old regime according to Heyking (second edition, page 14) " the consular archives enjoy inviolability, provided they are kept apart from any private correspondence." Under the decree of July 7, 1921 the Soviet government has provided that consular chancelleries may not be searched, examined, or sealed without the consent of the consul.

*Salvador:* The Salvadorean position on the inviolability of the archives of foreign consuls in Salvador is expressed in exactly the same terms as that of Honduras, *supra.* Articles 37 and 41 of the law on foreign consuls. Salvadorean consuls are instructed to claim inviolability of the archives as essential to their office. Regulations, 1905, art. 17; also organic law of the diplomatic and consular service, art. 93.

*Spain:* Toda y Guell (p. 35) and Maluquer y Salvador (p. 110) writing on the consular law of Spain agree that archives are inviolable.

*Sweden:* Article 36, as amplified by rule 84, of the *Swedish Consular Ordinance and Instructions* provides for the separation of official and private papers. " It is a rule generally recognized that the consular archives are inviolable, and that the local authorities cannot examine or seize them ". Rule 78.

*Texas:* Following article 10 of the general instructions sent out to American consuls in 1833, the Texas regulations required that the consular books be not mixed with those of the consul's private affairs.

*Turkey:* On November 11, 1914 the American ambassador at Constantinople cabled the Secretary of State that the Turkish authorities insisted on searching all consulates and everything therein except archives and requested the presence of consuls. A strong protest was immediately entered by the United States. It is interesting to note that the Turks did not claim to include archives in their search.

On December 4, 1914, local officials claiming to act under orders from the central government broke the American consular seal on the door of the room containing British and French consular archives and took those archives away. The ambassador was instructed to request the immediate return of the archives, an explanation, and assurances that the seal of the United States would not be violated in the future.

*Uruguay:* The regulations have consistently claimed the inviolability of the archives, which are to be kept separate from private papers. *Reglamento Consular,* 1878, art. 20; 1906, arts. 72, 321; 1917, arts. 57, 342.

*Venezuela:* The position of archives of foreign consuls in the Republic is defined after this fashion in article 3 of the decree of 1883:

> The chancelleries and the flag, shield, archives, and seals of each consulate are inviolable, and in no case can be occupied, registered, attached, or damaged, without the offender incurring to the fullest extent the responsibility which the laws fix for this offense.

The various editions of the consular regulations have placed the claims of Venezuelan consuls on a basis of reciprocity, so the above may be taken as a statement of the extent to which the Venezuelan government will go in supporting the claims of its consuls. Specific statement that the archives are the property of the state is to be found in the regulations of 1923, art. 33; 1921, art. 27; 1910, art. 48; 1905, art. 24. Regulations of 1905 (art. 31) and 1887 (art. 33) authorized Venezuelan consuls to claim inviolability of the archives.

*United States:* With regard to the consular archives all of the editions of the consular regulations have been in accord, both in requiring the separation of the consul's private books from the official records and in the assertion of a claim to inviolability of the latter. The first statement on the subject is found in the general instructions of 1833 in these words:

> Article 10. The consular books are not to be mixed with those of the consul's private affairs; and, his consular business should, if possible, be transacted in a separate apartment from that in which his ordinary commercial or other affairs are carried on. . . .

As section 62 of the general instructions of 1855 this read: "The consular books are to be kept distinct from those of the consul's private affairs . . . " which private affairs were to be conducted in a place separate from that which was indicated by the coat of arms as the consular office. " This provision was carried into the regulations of 1868 as section 452; 1870 and 1874 as section 418; 1881 as section 593; 1888 as section 593; and 1896 as section 609.

The inviolability of the consular archives first came into the regulations as section 12 of those of 1868, as follows:

> As a general rule, the records and papers of the consulate are inviolable, and under no pretext are they to be seized or examined by the local authorities. But this rule is by no means universally admitted, and the exemption is more frequently granted by treaty stipulation. In Great Britain the consular

property has been seized and held liable for the debt of a consul, for rent and taxes. (Citing Manchester newspapers, 1858, and de Clerq, *Guide Pratique.*)

In 1870 this was reduced to "The actual papers and archives of the consulate are exempt from seizure and detention" (section 22), which exact words were adopted by the regulations of 1874. The same idea was expressed in the regulations of 1881, section 77, "He may claim inviolability for the archives and official property of his office, and their exemption from seizure or examination". This expression was also adopted by the editions of 1888 (section 50) and 1896 (section 73).

Not only has this been the uniform stipulation for American consuls abroad, but it is believed that it has been uniformly applied toward foreign consuls in the United States. In 1862 Major General Butler, in command of the federal forces in New Orleans, had information which led him to believe that the Netherlands consul in that city had possession of funds belonging to the Confederacy. When the general sought to verify the information, the consul refused to give an explanation of the ownership of the money in question, hoisted the Netherlands' flag, and declared that he would stand on his consular privileges. General Butler refused to recognize these, had the consulate and the person of the consul searched, and ordered the official records of the consulate taken to the mint for safekeeping. It later developed that the funds in dispute were the property of a Netherlands firm. In apologizing for the conduct of the army officer, the Secretary of State wrote:

It appears, beyond dispute, that the person of the consul was unnecessarily and rudely searched; that certain papers, which incontestably were archives of the consulate, were seized and removed, and they are still withheld from him; and that he was not only denied the privilege of conferring with a friendly colleague, but was addressed in very discourteous and disrespectful language.

In these proceedings the military agents assumed functions which belong exclusively to the Department of State, acting under the directions of the President. Their conduct was a violation of the law of nations, and of the comity due from this country to a friendly sovereign state. The government disapproves of these proceedings . . . and expresses its regrets that the misconduct thus censured has occurred. (Seward, Sec. of State, to Van Limburg, June 5, 1862, *Foreign Relations,* 1863, p. 625.)

A most flagrant violation of the consular archives occurred at Saltillo, Mexico, in 1914 when not only the office records but also the official code book were removed. The case was further complicated, however, by the imprisonment of the American vice consul and his detention for several weeks under constant threat of execution. The entire proceeding was made the basis of a very vigorous protest by the State Department—a protest which resulted in the release of the consul, though there does not appear the result with regard to the archives. *Foreign Relations,* 1914, pp. 660-668.

In 1922 when no government of Mexico had been recognized by the United States, the Oliver American Trading Company brought suit against the unrecognized government and attached the archives and property of the Mexican consulate general in New York City. Though the individual acting as Mexican consul had not been so received by the United States, no objections to his acting as such had been interposed. The attachment resulted in the consulate having to suspend operations. In a communication to the governor of New York asking that the proper law officer of the state be asked to try to secure the release of the attachment, the Secretary of State on October 27, wrote that: "Under generally accepted practice and comity a consul may claim inviolability for the archives and official property of his office, and their exemption from seizure or examination, and the Department is of opinion that under existing circumstances the person acting as Mexican consul general in New York, even though he has received no exequatur, should in practice be accorded such inviolability." The attachment was dropped by consent.

Several cases in which the inviolability of the archives has been maintained in connection with the appearance of the consul as witness are cited *infra,* page 138. The following example is illustrative of the reasoning upon which this result is based:

The information regarding which your testimony is desired was communicated by Mr. Nickel to you in your capacity of consul general of the United States, and as such officer you took action and communicated the statements to the Department, thereby making them a part of the record of your consulate.

It is provided in Article V of the treaty of 1871 with Germany that the consular archives shall be at all times inviolable and where communications are from their nature confidential, for the cognizance of the consul's government only, it is clear that the consular officers should not be called upon to testify regarding them.

The Department, therefore, can not authorize you to testify in the case, on the ground that whatever knowledge you may have is official and privileged, because concerning only your relation to your own government. (Rockhill, Third Assistant Sec. of State, to Mr. Mason, July 31, 1894; Moore, *Digest,* V: 83. This position was again maintained in 1899: Hay, Sec. of State, to Mr. White, March 6, 1899; Moore, *Digest,* V: 82.)

Though this inviolability exists, there is little danger that it will be used to defeat the ends of justice in the state where the records are located. Thus in a case where the Mexican government brought suit against an individual for pillaging a church during a raid and desired the production of an invoice from the American consular files to prove the character of a certain shipment made soon after the raid, there is reason to believe that the United States authorized the production of the invoice.

A course somewhat similar to that pursued in cases where the consul as witness has been protected in his possession of official information was followed in a case where a Greek consul was made defendant in a suit to require him to deliver a commission from the Holy Synod of Greece appointing the pastor of the Community. When the Greek chargé called the attention of the Department of State to the suit and to the possible violation of the consular convention between the United States and Greece, the Department requested the Attorney General to have the United States district attorney intervene to show the opinion of the Department that the suit might be in violation of the provisions of the consular convention as well as "at variance with the principles of international law relative to the immunity of consular archives". The request was complied with. *Foreign Relations,* 1914, 326-330.

The net result of the different cases in which the rule has been invoked, as revealed by an examination of the published and unpublished records of the Department of State indicates the position of the Department to be that "the custom of regarding the official papers and archives of consulates as inviolable and exempt from seizure and examination by the authorities of the local government is so general and has been so frequently stipulated for in treaties" that inviolability may now be regarded as a right.

The provision securing inviolability for consular archives was one of the first to appear in American treaties affecting consuls and it has found a place in all such conventions. In all, forty-four treaties with thirty-two different states carry some statement on the matter. Those statements are not identical though the changes in phraseology are hardly of great importance since all seem to have served the purpose of protecting official papers. Differences are found in two respects: (a) the persons against whom the prohibitions are applicable, and (b) the exact acts which are prohibited. Viewed in this light the treaty stipulations group themselves in this manner:

1. Full and entire immunity for chancery and papers therein.
   France, CC, 1788: II.
2. Archives protected from all examinations.
   Sweden and Norway, A&C, 1816: V.
3. Archives and documents exempt from (b) all search.
   Sweden and Norway, C&N, 1827: XIII.
   Greece, C&N, 1837: XII.
4. Archives and papers respected inviolably; under no pretext can (a) any magistrate (b) seize or interfere with them.
   Colombia, AC&N, 1824: XXVIII.
   Central America, PAC&N, 1825: XXX.
   Denmark, FC&N, 1826: X.
   Brazil, AC&N, 1828: XXX.
   Mexico, AC&N, 1831: XXIX.
   Chile, PAC&N, 1832: XXVIII.
   Venezuela, PAC&N, 1836: XXXI.
   Ecuador, PFN&C, 1839: XXXI.
   Portugal, C&N, 1840: X.
   Colombia, PAN&C, 1846: XXXII.
   Guatemala, PFC&N, 1849: XXX.
   Salvador, AN&C, 1850: XXXII.
   Bolivia, PFC&N, 1858: XXXIII.
5. Archives and papers respected inviolably; under no pretext can (a) any magistrate or any other person (b) seize or interfere with them.
   Peru-Bolivia, PFC&N, 1836: XXVII.

6. Archives and papers respected inviolably; under no pretext can (a) any functionary (b) seize or interfere with them.
   Colombia, CC, 1850: V.
7. Archives and papers respected inviolably; under no pretext can (a) any magistrate or any other functionary (b) visit, seize, or interfere with them.
   Switzerland, FC&E, 1850: VII.
8. Archives and papers respected inviolably; under no pretext can (a) any magistrate or any other functionary (b) inspect, seize, or interfere with them.
   Orange Free State, FC&E, 1871: V.
9. Archives and papers respected inviolably; under no pretext can (a) any person, magistrate, or other public authority (b) interfere with or seize them.
   Peru, FC&N, 1851: XXXVI; FC&N, 1870, XXXIII; FC&N, 1887: XXI.[1]
   Haiti, ACN&E, 1864: XXXV.
10. Archives and papers respected inviolably; under no pretext can (a) any magistrate or any of the local authorities (b) interfere with or seize them.
    Argentina, FC&N, 1853: XI.
11. Consular offices and dwellings inviolable, local authorities not to invade under any pretext. In no case may (a) local authorities (b) examine or seize papers there deposited.
    France, CC, 1853: III.
    Belgium, CC, 1868: VI.
    Italy, CC, 1868: VI.
    Salvador, AC&CP, 1870: XXXV.
    Austria-Hungary, CC, 1870: V.
12. Consular office inviolable, local authorities not to invade under any pretext. In no case may (a) local authorities (b) examine or seize papers there deposited.
    Belgium, CC, 1870: VI.
    Congo, AC&N, 1891: V.

[1] See Moore, *Digest*, V: 52 for an application of this provision.

Greece, CC, 1902: VI.
Servia, CC, 1891: VI.
Roumania, CC, 1881: VI.

13. Consular office inviolable, local authorities not to invade under any pretext. In no case may (a) local authorities (b) examine or sequestrate papers therein.
Italy, CC, 1878: VI.

14. Archives inviolable; under no pretence may (a) local authorities (b) examine or seize them.
German Empire, CC, 1871: V.[1]
Netherlands, CC, 1878: VI.

15. Consular office and archives inviolable; under no pretext may (a) local authorities (b) examine or take possession of official papers.
Spain, F&GR, 1902: XVIII.

16. Consular office and archives inviolable; under no pretext may (a) local authorities (b) examine or seize papers or compel consul to testify as to contents.
Sweden, CC, 1910: VI.

17. Archives and documents protected against all search; under no pretext may (a) any authority or magistrate (b) visit, seize, or examine (or search) them.
Netherlands, CC (colonies), 1855: V.

18. Consular offices and archives at all times inviolable; under no circumstances to be subjected to invasion by any authorities of any character. Nor shall (a) the authorities (b) make any seizure or examination of papers or property within office. No consular officer to be compelled to produce archives in court or testify as to their contents.
Germany, AC&CR, 1923: XX.

19. When the consul is a citizen of the receiving nation, he is to remain subject to its laws, but this shall not affect the inviolability of the consular archives.
Two Sicilies, ACN&E, 1855: XVIII.
Venezuela, ACN&E, 1860: XXVI.

[1] Applied in Kessler *v.* Best (1903), 121 Fed. 439. For an application when the consul is a witness, see Moore, *Digest*, V: 82, 83.

Many of the treaties (in general, those after 1860) provide specifically that official and private papers must be kept separated. As shown above, this is the position of the Department of State in the absence of treaty.

The matter of inviolability of consular archives is covered more completely by treaty than is any other of the consular privileges. While inviolability of the archives may clearly be claimed under international law, it is only the exceptional case where an American consul would have to rest his claim solely upon that. Some one of the above statements in treaties will be found to be applicable, either directly or by virtue of the most-favored-nation clause. Though the statements vary slightly in exact phrasing, the object in each case is to state a complete immunity; and it would seem that each of the provisions is sufficient to secure that.

As the treaty of friendship, commerce and consular rights with Germany is the latest expression of this immunity, it might be well to look into the extent as set out there. The consular archives are at all times inviolable. While within the consular office, the archives are protected by its inviolability as well as their own. Should a portion of the archives be removed for any reason, their inviolability would accompany them. No authorities may under any pretext make any examination or seizure of the papers; such a statement is sufficient to protect not only the papers themselves but also the information which they contain. While the inviolability of the archives has been interpreted to protect the papers and their contents against a subpoena issuing from a local court, the present treaty doubly insures that protection by specific provision. It is to be noted that nothing is said about the separation of official and private papers; that was felt to be a matter of domestic regulation to be covered by instructions issued to the consul by his government, and not a matter for negotiation between two states.

# CHAPTER III

## Display of the National Insignia, Position of the Consulate, and the Question of Asylum

One clearly defined group of privileges which have at times been claimed centers around the buildings in which the consular office and dwelling are located. In its broadest form this consists of a claim that the consular office is inviolable; and this inviolability has been claimed upon occasions when the consulate has been used as a place of asylum. In a more modified form it consists of a claim of a right to fly the national flag and to place an inscription on the door of the consulate, together with a right to a certain "respect" for the office; and to the more substantial privilege of inviolability of the consular archives. These items are sufficiently distinct to warrant a separate study of each.

### DISPLAY OF THE NATIONAL FLAG AND ARMS

Texts usually state that the display of the national flag and the use of an inscription indicating the nature of the consular office are secured to consuls by custom; and almost uniformly treaty provisions guarantee this privilege. The use of some means to designate the consular office is imperative; and the practice of using the national coat of arms and the inscription "Consulate of ——" (or its equivalent) has developed. So general is the practice and so necessary is it, that it may be said to have a basis in international law. The display of the flag, however, rests upon different grounds. Some text writers claim that this latter is a right which the consul is entitled to enjoy; and it must be admitted that there is a basis for such a statement in occasional official documents. Others more correctly contend that it is simply a privilege depending for its validity upon the practice in the district in which the consulate is situated. Such practice varies not only from state to state, but also from district to district within the particular state; for this reason it is impossible to state categorically that all consuls in any one state are, or are not, privileged to hoist the national flag. However, it is possible to note two points in connection with the display of the national insignia: the purpose for which the national flag may be raised, and the occasions upon which the display may be made.

As to the first of these it may be noted that the governments of the world in instructing their consular representatives on the point seem to confine themselves to three reasons: to indicate the location of the consular establishment, to afford protection to the consular office, and more properly to observe the holidays and days of mourning both of their native state and of the state of their residence.

According to a large number of consular regulations the occasions upon which the flag is to be hoisted are indicated in the third reason advanced for the act; in addition reference is sometimes made to the right in times of emergency, as in case of riot or insurrection. This limitation upon the times at which the flag can be flown nullifies the first reason advanced for the use of the flag. A prominent display of the national flag would serve as an effective guide to the consular office, and would in many cases make it easier for persons of the consul's state to locate that office; but it can hardly be contended that such a fact is more compelling upon a national holiday than upon other days. The very limiting of the occasions upon which the flag can be flown shows that the real reason for the display is not to mark the location of the consulate. Courtesy makes it a splendid gesture for a consul to display the flag of his state upon the holidays of that in which he resides; but if the display of the flag is substantially to benefit the consul, a more regular display would seem desirable. That the privilege is deemed important is shown by the frequency with which treaty provisions governing it are made, and by the protests that have been forthcoming over attempts at its suppression.

Of course, it is in order for the consul to raise the national flag in case of riot or insurrection, in order to mark out distinctly the location of the consulate to prevent its unwittingly being brought into the line of fire or made the object of an attack by either of the opposing parties.

The flag and the coat of arms are entitled to respect, and actions of the inhabitants of the district which involve disrespect of either of these are almost invariably followed by expressions of regret and often by reparations made by the government within whose jurisdiction the consulate is located.[1]

[1] "On October 19, 1888 the coat of arms of the German consulate at Havre was torn down and thrown into the public street from which the police brought it to the consulate, but the consul refused to receive it and brought his protest before the local authorities who communicated it to their superiors. The point was treated in Paris between the Ministry of Foreign Affairs and the German ambassador who arranged without difficulty the reparation due. On November 3 the coat of arms was replaced in the presence of the German consul by the French authorities." (Guesalaga, *Derecho Diplomático y Consular con los Últimos Casos de Controversias entre los Estados*, pp. 175, 176.)

In 1905 the coat of arms of the American consulate at Cienfuegos was besmeared. In reply to the American protest, the Cuban ambassador apologized for his government, expressing sincerest regrets and stating that the outrage was evidently committed by some persons endeavoring to alienate the United States and Cuba. *Foreign Relations*, 1905, pp. 288-290. A similar occurrence in 1904 had likewise brought an apology and a promise of a search for the instigators. *Ibid.*, 1904, 237.

On July 4, 1913 the Mexican consulate at Nogales, Arizona, displayed the Mexican flag in honor of American independence. Unknown persons removed the Mexican emblem and substituted for it that of the United States. In accordance with a note from the Mexican chargé calling his attention to the facts, the Secretary of State on July 7 started an investigation to determine whether Arizona officials were endeavoring to apprehend and punish the guilty persons.

The position of various states with regard to the display of the national insignia is shown by the following extracts from official documents:

*Argentina:* The hoisting of the national flag is authorized on the holidays of the Argentine Republic and of the state in which the consulate is located, in case of war or blockade, and at other times when practice authorizes, but at all times in accordance with established usage. *Reglamento Consular,* 1906, articles 381, 386.

*Austria-Hungary:* In reply to a foreign consul's request for information whether he was subject to local jurisdiction, the government of Trieste stated on December 12, 1831 that he was, adding:

Nevertheless, there pertains to foreign consuls, by a custom already received and constantly observed, the privilege of placing on their habitation the arms of their sovereign, and of wearing the uniform which comports with their rank. (Bursotti, *Guide des Agents Consulaires.*)

*Bolivia:* "Consuls general, consuls, and vice consuls will be subject with respect to . . . the coat of arms and the national flag, to customary law." *Reglamento Consular,* 1877, art. 18. The regulations of 1887, art. 21 consider as one of the attributes of consuls the placing of the coat of arms over the door and the flying of the national flag "on the days of custom".

*Chile:* The following appears in the regulations of 1897 and is taken over almost verbatim as articles 121 and 122 of the regulations of 1915:

Article 38. Always when the treaties, laws or usages of the country permit, they will place over the door of the consular office the coat of arms of the Republic with the inscription "Consulate general", "Consulate", or "Vice consulate of Chile". Likewise they will raise the national flag on the anniversaries of national fiestas of the country, and will place it at half mast on days of public mourning, scrupulously observing the established usage of the country.

Article 39. The coat of arms and the national flag have solely as their object to indicate the residence of the consular employees; but it is never to be understood that the consular dwelling or office can give asylum to any criminals, even though they be Chilean citizens, nor obstruct the speed of citation or execution of the justice of the country.

The object specified in article 39 would be equally applicable to the practice of daily display of the national flag; but the action of the executive in placing the object in article 39 in connection with a denial of any claim to the right of asylum, rather than in article 28 where certain occasions for the display of the flag are listed, would indicate that the effect desired was not a statement of purpose but a limitation upon the immunity which might be claimed as a result of the display.

*Colombia:* A *memoria* presented to Congress in 1845 contained an extract from a circular distributed to the diplomatic corps at Bogotá and an explanation thereof by the secretary of foreign relations:

"Foreign consuls not having a diplomatic character, the custom of hoisting their national flag can not give them one, nor signify anything other than the location of their dwellings. The executive power does not find it inconvenient to permit, for the present, in the ports of the Republic, the custom which has been introduced into them of flying the flags to designate to the ships and the subjects of the different nations the dwellings of their consuls; without intending that these signs should withdraw the buildings on which they are placed, from the jurisdiction of the country nor from the searches of the local authorities."

With perfect right this custom introduced gradually into New

Granada might have been prohibited, since the law of nations does not authorize consuls to use this insignia, nor is the custom general; but it is believed that it will not be inconvenient expressly to authorize it as a custom equivalent to and more visible than the tablet which consuls have previously used in some countries over the door of their habitations, but explaining clearly what this signifies. (Uribe, *Anales Diplomáticos y Consulares de Colombia,* III: 169.)

Apparently the daily flying of the flag is permissible under this authority, but only as a privilege, not as a right.

The *Guía Consular de la República de Colombia,* p. 30, contains almost the same phraseology as the Chilean regulations, *supra.*

*Congo:* " International usage authorizes consuls to place the coat of arms of their nation outside their offices and to raise their national flag." Relations with Foreign Consuls, art. 3, contained in *Foreign Relations,* 1887, 26-29.

*Costa Rica:* Articles 25, 26, and 33 of the consular regulations of 1888 made the display of the flag dependent upon the customs of the locality, and indicated the days upon which consuls normally might expect to make use of the privilege. The provision of the law of 1920, article 12, is that " on it (the consulate) will be placed the coat of arms of the Republic with the proper inscription and also the pole for the hoisting of the flag on national holidays and the usual days of the country of residence."

*Denmark:* Paragraphs 47 and 80 of the *Instructions pour les Consuls de Danemark à l'Étranger* place the use of the flag by Danish consuls on the footing of usage. While a notification of the Danish minister of justice forbids the flying of flags other than Danish within that country, "the prohibition does not include the ministers, consuls, or vice consuls of foreign states. These are entitled to hoist the flag which concerns them before their offices in this country as well as before the residences of the ministers. . . . " *International Law Situations,* 1917, 83.

*Dominican Republic:* Consuls are to display the national insignia " as a sign of their functions and protection with respect to their compatriots " on specified occasions in conformity with custom. *Ley Orgánica de la Cuerpo Consular de la República Dominicana,* art. 9.

*Ecuador:* An executive decree of November 7, 1900 provides in article 7 for the placing of the coat of arms and an inscription on the outside of the consulate, but does not mention the national flag. *Leyes, Decretos Legislativos y Ejecutivos Reglamentos . . . Relacionades con el Servicio Diplomático y Consular del Ecuador* (1917), p. 47.

*France:* The British consul at Havre reported on Dec. 1, 1871 that " the right to display a flag or coat of arms " was conceded him by custom. *Reports relative to British Consular Establishments,* I: 124.

*Germany:* The imperial coat of arms might be used by German consuls " whenever admissible by custom and law " under the general instructions of 1872 (page 10).

*Great Britain:* The following sentence is taken from a letter from Consul Cameron to the King of Abssynia: " As regards a consul's flying a flag, this is by no means necessary; nor would my Government even wish it, if, as I hear, your people might misunderstand it ". Although the consul was severely criticized by his government for his actions in other respects, the above statement was not questioned. *British State Papers,* Vol. 53, p. 61. The *Foreign Office List* for 1924 contains at page 101 a list of occasions upon which the flag should be hoisted, and these are all days having a public significance. Nothing is said about the display of the flag at any other time.

*Guatemala:* " They may raise the flag and place the coat of arms of the nation which they represent over the door if there is no law or custom to the contrary, in the country of their residence." *Apéndice al Reglamento Diplomático y Consular de la República,* par. 6.

*Hawaii:* Public occasions and Hawaiian holidays were to be observed by the display of the Hawaiian flag. Regulations of 1895, art. 40.

*Honduras:* Article 37 of the law on foreign consuls in Honduras provides that:

> On the outside of the houses the consular officers may place an inscription which expresses the character, category, and consular charge. For better guarantee in case of outbreak of any mutiny or rebellion, or in case of war, they may hoist the flag of their country.

This would seem to limit the display of the flag to cases of emergency. The action of Honduranean consuls abroad is governed by article 34 of the regulations of 1906 which is similar to article 38 of the Chilean regulations of 1897, and only mentions the unfurling of the flag on the national holidays in accordance with local custom. A strict interpretation of the law on foreign consuls would not be in accordance with the principle of reciprocity.

*Liberia:* International usage is made to govern the display of the Liberian flag by articles 25 and 26 of the consular regulations.

*Mexico:* Early in its national life the republic forbade consuls to display the flag of their state, a presidential decree of August 23, 1828 accomplishing this. The attention of the ministry of foreign relations having been called to the fact that the decree referred to had been violated by the flying of consular flags in the city of Vera Cruz on national holidays, a circular of September 4, 1830 advised that flag staffs be not kept on the dwellings of consuls. *Derecho Internacional Mexicano,* III: 142, 143.

In 1859 a law governing the position of foreign consuls within the national borders was passed; under the terms of article 30 of that statute, "Commercial agents may place on the outside of the buildings an inscription which expresses the official character and nationality. The flag of their country will be hoisted only when the city in which they reside is besieged or some revolution or sedition breaks out in its vicinity." Apparently, however, no express authorization was given to restore flag poles which were to have been destroyed under the circular of 1830.

Some light is thrown on the manner of the enforcement of this provision of the law of 1859 (which is still in force) by a despatch from an American consul in Mexico to the Secretary of State in 1874. From that it seems that the *jefe político* at Tuxpan had denied the consul the right to display the American flag on public holidays and feast days as contrary to the provisions of the law governing the subject; though at the same time he expressed the opinion that the president of the republic would grant the desired permission. When the president was appealed to, he declined to comply with the request on the ground that it was not within his power to authorize the violation of a law; however, he added that the government had never enforced observance of the provision. *Foreign Relations,* 1874, p. 719.

Some years later a very different interpretation was placed upon the same provision, when the American consul at Mazatlan requested permission to display the American flag on Washington's birthday. The request which was originally addressed to the governor of Sinaloa was forwarded by the latter to the secretary of foreign relations.

The advice which was transmitted from this office was that the prohibition on foreign consuls contained in article 30 of the law of November 26, 1859 does not imply not giving them permission to raise the flag of their respective countries in cases authorized by international usage, provided that in the opinion of the local authority, there be no special motive of public order which would impede it; but that such permission belongs to this department to give; that in the case proposed by the governor of Sinaloa there being no inconvenience of the nature indicated, the said governor was authorized to grant the license which he requested.

In June of the same year (1895) general authorization was given to the said governor in order that in similar cases he might concede permits to other consuls, communicating to this department in each case the permit which he grants. (*Guía Diplomática y Consular*, 249-251.)

The effect of the new interpretation was to place Mexico on the same footing with other states which left the matter to local usage—with the exception of the fact that there still remained a possibility of central control, and that each case might have to be made the subject of a special application.

In a note to the Secretary of State of the United States under date of March 30, 1912, the Mexican ambassador maintained that the display of the national flag was not a matter of right, and cited in support of his position extracts from an opinion of the legal officer of the Mexican Ministry of Foreign Affairs which in turn relied on expressions contained in the consular regulations of the United States and official communications of the Secretary of State.[1]

The position to be maintained by Mexican consular officers abroad was thus expressed by article 100 of the regulations of 1871: "The use of the Mexican flag over the house and office will be subject to the prescriptions or permissions of the regulations and uses of the country of the consular district"—a position thoroughly consistent with the provisions of the law of 1859. *Derecho Internacional Mexicano*, III: 192.

[1] See *infra*, p. 78.

The consular regulations of 1923 for the guidance of Mexican consular officers in foreign countries provide that the national flag is to be hoisted on national holidays and days of mourning and on days established by the customs of the place in which the consulate is located—which would indicate that the government had not accepted the contention of the United States that the use of the national flag is a matter of right. *Reglamento de la Ley Orgánica del Servicio Mexicano,* art. 22. These regulations state that local legislation and custom in certain countries permit the display of the national flag on the occasions indicated (art. 55B), but that the shield may be affixed to the consular office by virtue of a right established in international law (art. 53D).

*Netherlands:* The *Netherlands Consular Service Rules and Regulations* of 1908 accord with the instructions issued in 1902 based on the regulations of 1874 in recognizing that the consular officer is " entitled " to place the arms of the kingdom over the door of the consulate and may display the flag; but with regard to the coat of arms

> he must, however, bear in mind that this permission has for object only the convenience of the Netherlands subjects and by no means intends to elevate the consulate into a place of refuge in the countries where such act is at variance with laws or custom.

Nothing is said of the occasions upon which the flag may be displayed; and it is impossible to tell from the quotation whether the " permission " referred to is that of the Netherlands government or of the government near which the consul resides.

*Panama:* Law 78 of 1904 refers to the coat of arms and the national flag " which are used to indicate the location of the consular office ".

*Paraguay:* Under the regulations of 1871:

Art. 13. The consuls of the Republic of Paraguay will employ the national coat of arms, in accordance with custom, on all solemn and festive holidays, and will hoist the flag of the Republic in case of social or civil disturbances, always respecting the laws of the country to which they are accredited.

Art. 53. In case of the death of the sovereign, prince, or chief of the country in which they reside, they shall . . . hoist their flags at half mast.

Thus the display of the insignia seems to be authorized only on special occasions and in time of disturbance, and always to be subject to local regulation.

*Persia:* Articles 17 and 18 of the regulations in force contain an authorization of the use of insignia, but do not go into detail as to the time of use.

*Peru:* The provisions of the Chilean regulations set out above are almost identical with those of the Peruvian regulations of 1897 (articles 231 and 232), except that the latter specifically note that war or blockade will constitute an occasion for the display of the national flag. The provisions of the earlier editions of consular regulations were similar; see those of 1863 (art. 44) and 1888 (arts. 263, 264).

*Russia:* The provisions of the Russian consular regulations were thus paraphrased by Baron Heyking in his *Practical Guide for Russian Consular Officers:*

According to article 15 of the Russian consular regulations the consular flag may only be hoisted on rowing boats and in ports where the consul has his permanent residence. From this it appears that consular officers are not entitled to hoist the flag in ports where they only reside temporarily. The article in question further permits them, to hoist the flag, if the local authorities have no objection, on the house where they reside. If, therefore, at the place of residence of the consular officer it is not the custom to hoist consular flags on houses, he must refrain from doing so. (Page 11.)

To this statement the second edition adds: "The Russian flag must be hoisted on Russian as well as on local holidays".

Consuls might exhibit the national coat of arms on their houses according to the report of the British consul at Taganrog on Dec. 1, 1871. *Reports relative to British Consular Establishments,* II: 126.

"Consuls have the right to put up on the door the coat of arms of their country and the inscription 'Consulate' . . . of such a country, and their national flag." Summary of a decree of the Soviet Government published in the Moscow *Isvestia* for July 7, 1921.

*Salvador:* The phraseology of the Salvadorean law on foreign consuls differs only slightly from that of the Honduranean law on the same subject. Article 39 provides that:

> On the outside of the houses the consular officers may place an inscription which expresses the character and category of the consular charge, and the nationality. For better guarantee in case of the outbreak of any mutiny or rebellion, or in case of invasion or foreign war, they may hoist the flag of their country.

This is amplified by the decree of Feb. 1, 1908 to the effect

> . . . that international law only concedes to diplomatic and consular agents the right to place on their houses the flag and shield of their countries to indicate to the public and to the authorities the international character with which they are invested. . . . (Ramirez Pena, *Cartilla Consular,* sec. 38.)

The same remarks made about the Chilean statement are applicable here; namely, that the purpose of the decree is merely to deny any claim of a right of asylum, not to extend the list of occasions upon which the flag may be hoisted.

*South African Republic:* The statement of article 4 of the regulations issued in 1895 have only slight verbal differences from the Netherlands regulations *supra.*

*Spain:* As early as 1765 Charles III issued a decree on foreign consuls, the relevant part of which was:

The houses of consuls do not enjoy any immunity, and they can not place on the exterior part of the house the arms of the Prince of the state which names them; they can only place on their towers or terraces or in any other part of their house a sign which makes known to the individuals of their nation the house of the consul. (Bursotti, *Guide des Agents Consulaires,* I: 208.)

The last part of the quotation was interpreted by several foreign consuls to mean that they might display their national flag; and on a holiday of his country, the Dutch consul displayed the flag of the Netherlands. An immediate protest was forthcoming from the local officials and the matter was taken to the king. It pleased his majesty to decree that consuls should use no other insignia than that provided, which was a standard sign for all consuls, with the name of the country underneath—a usage which did not become established. See Wertheim, *Manuel à l'Usage des Consuls des Pays-Bas,* II: 285.

Antonio de Castro y Casaleiz notes in his *Guía Práctica del Diplomático Español* (Vol. I, page 858) a royal ordinance of November 3, 1851 permitting foreign consuls to raise the flag of their state over their houses.

*Sweden:* Every consul must possess the Swedish flag and coat of arms, and the latter should be " affixed to his place of office, where suitable, to indicate his premises ". Article 37, *Swedish Consular Ordinance and Instructions.* No mention is made of the display of the flag.

The coat of arms of the kingdom is to be affixed at every consulate, which, however, does not include legation offices. As the purpose of this stipulation is to facilitate callers in finding the consulate, the coat of arms ought to be placed on the outside of the house containing the consulate in a manner to make it easily seen. (Rule 87.)

*Switzerland:* The consul may place arms on the door of the consulate when conventions or laws do not oppose. Regulations, art. 86.

*Texas:* The regulations issued by Texas as an independent republic closely resembled those of the United States; and article 10 dealing with the use of the arms of the republic was identical with article 10 of the instructions issued to American consuls in 1833.

*Uruguay:* The subject was dismissed in the regulations of 1878 (articles 53, 54) with the injunction to the consuls to follow the usage of the district. As amended in 1907 (article 81) and 1917 (article 66) the regulations still consider usage as governing in the absence of treaty, but the national holidays of Uruguay and of the state of residence, the case of war or blockade, and days of mourning are suggested as the times upon which the flag should be hoisted.

*Venezuela:* Article 4 of the decree of January 25, 1883 defining the position of foreign consuls in the Republic is as follows:

> The said flag, which on solemn occasions may be flown over the places of their habitation, and the shield which they may fix on the outer doors of these same buildings, do not signify any right of asylum, exemption, or privilege which withdraws the person, the house, or those found in it, from the common law and jurisdiction of the territory.

This provision limits the custom to "solemn occasions"; the regulations governing the action of Venezuelan consuls abroad are a little more extended:

> Consuls will raise the Venezuelan flag on the national holidays of the Republic, during the time a ship of the national

navy is in the port, and on those days on which it is a custom in the place of their residence, and will place it at half mast on days of public mourning. (Regulations of 1923, art. 28, adopting the language of the regulations of 1921, art. 22, and 1922, art. 41.)

The provisions of the earlier regulations had been similar. See those of 1905, article 39; 1885, article 38; and 1865, article 22.

*United States:* In this respect the present position of the United States represents a considerable development from the position first taken—a development which has gone so far as perhaps to place the United States in a more advanced position than that maintained by most states. The first reference to the use of insignia near the consulates seems to have been in the General Instructions sent out in 1833, and that is merely to the effect that "it (the apartment in which the consul transacts official business) must be designated by the arms of the United States exhibited at the entrance, and the words 'Consulate of the United States' in English, and in the language of the country where the consul resides" (Article 10). There is no mention whatever of a consular flag. A similar provision has been incorporated into each revision of the instructions and regulations issued since that time. General Instructions, 1855, sec. 62; *Consular Regulations,* 1868, sec. 454; 1870, sec. 418; 1874, sec. 62; 1881, sec. 593; 1888, sec. 593; 1896, sec. 609.

The general instructions of 1855 were the first to incorporate a provision concerning the flag. Section 30 of that compilation authorized the consul to display the arms and flag "as signs of his authority" wherever such custom prevailed. The flag was to be unfurled on the national holidays; and in accordance with custom upon the approach and in the presence of an American vessel and upon the death of any American ship-master or distinguished citizen within the consulate, or of a public officer at home. The proper interpretation of the provision seems to be that custom is to control; if custom permits, the consul may use the flag as a sign of his authority by its display every day should he think such action necessary or advisable; but if custom is more restricted and applies only on stated occasions, then those mentioned in section 30 are to be taken as proper.

Such an interpretation is directly in line with section 360 of the *Consular Regulations* of 1868 which in addition to listing certain public occasions upon which the flag should be unfurled, stated that "wherever such custom prevails, the national flag should be hoisted daily for his protection, and as the emblem of his authority". Thus the consular officer was explicitly directed to display the flag each day if custom permitted; and the unqualified manner of making the statement seems to indicate that such a proceeding would not be considered as unusual. The provisions of the Regulations of 1870 (section 74) and 1874 (section 74) are almost identical with those just cited; but the edition of 1881 brought an additional statement on the point. According to section 134:

> The arms of the United States should be placed over the entrance of the consulate or commercial agency, unless prohibited by the laws of the country. Wherever the custom prevails, the national flag should be hoisted on such occasions as the consular officer may deem appropriate, or when it may be required for his protection, or as the emblem of his authority. It is not usually necessary that it should be unfurled daily. The occasions for its display are within the judgment of the consular officer; but its use will be suggested on all national holidays of his own country, and whenever it would indicate a becoming respect to the customs, festivals, or public ceremonies of the country to which he is accredited.

This phraseology, apparently calculated to forestall exaggerated claims on the part of consuls, was adopted by the Regulations of 1888, the only change in the paragraph being a specification of the place of use of the national arms in the added sentence, " Only one coat-of-arms will be permitted to be exposed in each port where a consular office is located, and that, of course, will be placed over the office devoted to consular business ". The provisions of the Regulations of 1888 (section 110) were carried into those of 1896 (section 70), and were left untouched by the revision of 1923.

A supplementary statement found in the Regulations from 1881 to the present provides that " Permission to display the national flag is not a matter of right, though it is usually accorded, and it is often provided for by treaty ". Regulations, 1881, sec. 77; 1888, sec. 50; 1896, sec. 73.

Yet the fact that the revision of 1923 makes no changes on this point does not necessarily mean that there had been no alteration of the position taken by the United States between the time of the adoption of the Regulations of 1881 and that of the revision of 1923. As was clearly the case in earlier editions, the emphasis was on functions; and the particular statement under consideration did not warrant any special study. Treaty provisions had given an unqualified right to display the flag in many cases [1] and diplomatic negotiations had given opportunity for a considered view of the position.

In reply to the despatch mentioned above [2] in which an American consul reported the refusal of the Mexican president to issue a permit which would violate the terms of the law of 1859, the Secretary of State wrote that the matter was one subject to municipal law [3]—a view which was sustained in instructions given by the Assistant Secretary of State to Mr. Barron on October 20, 1897.

[1] See *infra*, pp. 95-101.

[2] *Supra*, p. 68.

[3] *Foreign Relations*, 1874, p. 730.

In 1912 the Mexican law of 1859 was again made the subject of correspondence between the diplomatic branches of the American and Mexican governments, and on that occasion the matter of the display of the national flag was studied *de novo.* The note of the Secretary of State to the Mexican ambassador under date of June 21, 1912 may be taken as the latest definitive statement of the position of the United States on the legal right to fly the flag; and that statement shows a considerable variation from that enunciated in the *Consular Regulations,* as the following extract will indicate:

Concerning the flying of the national flag as a question of right, the Department, after a very careful consideration, feels quite sure that a reexamination of the authorities upon international law by the proper Mexican legal officers will convince your Excellency's Government that the display by a consul of the flag of his country is a thing which may be properly claimed as a right under international law and that the Mexican Government, by its practice in permitting the consul to display the flag on the national holiday of this country, and the legal adviser of the Mexican Foreign Office, in the present instance by so recommending, appear to recognize this, notwithstanding the Mexican municipal law of 1859 cited by your Excellency, which provides that commercial agents residing in Mexico may display the flags of their countries only when the town where they reside is besieged, or when a riot or sedition breaks out therein.

This Department is aware that the extent to which the right to display the flag can be exercised is variously stated; that some authorities limit it to solemn occasions and some to national holidays, while others merely state the right without limiting it. But since the reason for displaying the flag above the consular premises as recognized in international law is, as expressed in the consular treaties of the United States with other countries "in order that the consular office or dwelling may be easily and generally known for the convenience of those who may resort to them," [1] it would seem that the flag of the consul's nation might be displayed at all times and not merely on certain holidays. And indeed this is the course that has been followed by American consuls at various places throughout the world, who, basing their action upon this ground, do now, as they have done in the past, daily display the national flag. This is likewise, it would appear, the practice of other nations.

. . . this Government . . . hopes that . . . the former (Mexican) Government will see fit fully to recognize the rules and principles of international law governing this matter and to refrain from insisting upon a strict compliance by American consuls with the provisions of the Mexican law of 1859 with regard to the matter, thus permitting them to display the American flag in such manner and at such times as their discretion dictates, unless in particular cases some good reason exists and can be shown why this should not be done. (*Foreign Relations*, 1912, p. 902.)

Two departures from previous practice are to be found in the above note. The first is with reference to the display of the national flag as a matter of right. Since no authorities are cited and no attempt is made to distinguish the earlier position, it is impossible to determine whether the Department's new attitude is based on a development in international law or upon an admission that the earlier stand was incorrect and therefore should be reversed. However advisable the departmental position may be in practice, it is believed that the earlier communications of the Department more nearly coincide with the practice of states as well as the opinions of the writers.

The second departure comes with reference to the limitation upon the times at which the flag may be displayed. As noted above the provisions of the Consular Regulations issued from time to time had not been uniform in this respect,

[1] This language is to be found in only two treaties. See *infra*, p. 96.

while the latest edition of the Regulations had indicated that a daily display of the flag was usually unnecessary. The note of 1912 does not expressly claim a right to unfurl the flag every day though from the reason for displaying the flag " it would seem that the flag of the consul's nation might be displayed at all times "; and such appears to be the practice of nations. As to the latter point judgment requires a knowledge of the practice of many states in many localities—information which the Department of State might very well have at its disposal. The reason advanced for the alleged right is a logical one and no doubt is conclusive as to those states with which the United States has treaties; but there was no governing treaty provision between the United States and Mexico, and whether the reason advanced really has its basis in international law is at least open to question. That the practice of flying the national flag over consulates antedated treaty provisions on the subject is clear; that such practice was not indulged in daily is indicated by the almost uniform provisions of consular regulations which may be taken as formulations of existing practice, not as innovations. The further fact that the days mentioned are always days having a public significance is persuasive that the indulgence was considered a matter of courtesy, without a utilitarian aspect. In view of these considerations it is probable that the reason advanced is not sustained historically. In any event it would be difficult to reconcile the earlier instructions regarding the practice with the reason advanced in 1912 for that practice.

Nevertheless, the position of the United States today must be taken as one declaring the display of the national insignia to be a matter of right, to be exercised by the consul at his discretion unless a good reason can be given by the local authorities why, in a particular instance, the right should not be used.

American treaty provisions will be found at the end of this chapter.

INVIOLABILITY OF THE CONSULATE

Perhaps the most conclusive answer to the statement made by some writers that the consulate is inviolable is that, with rare exceptions, the governments of the world have not claimed such an immunity in the absence of treaty. A fair test of this is afforded by a consideration of the provisions of consular regulations which in most cases give the consul information as to what privileges he may claim to enjoy by virtue of his position; in the lists thus set out, a claim for the inviolability of the consulate is not included. On the contrary it is the practice of most governments to condemn the use of the consulate as an asylum (for the provisions on this point see the subdivision next succeeding) and in so doing to state that the consulate and its contents can not be withdrawn from the local jurisdiction; and a few have gone to the point of making specific denials in addition to this.[1]

[1] "In 1879 an officer of the Mexican government exacted a forced loan from various persons, including Macmanus and Sons, an American firm, of which Mr. Scott, the American consul at Chihuahua, was a member. The consular office, it appears, was used as a place of deposit for the funds of American citizens engaged in business in Chihuahua; and, when payment was demanded, Mr. Scott closed the doors. An officer later appeared with an additional force, when Mr. Scott, concluding that further resistance was useless opened the door, and the officer obtained the sum required. Even supposing, said Mr. Evarts, that the consul had been engaged in no other business than that of an official character, there was nothing in the treaty of 1831 which guaranteed to his place of business freedom from search. There was a distinct guarantee of the archives and papers of the consulate, but it was not alleged that these were disturbed. By a stipulation in the treaty the parties had agreed to enter into a special convention for defining the powers and immunities of consuls, but all attempts in that direction had proved abortive, so that no exemption of the offices of consuls from being entered by the authorities of the country could be claimed as a right, especially where a consular officer was a member of a mercantile firm and his place of business was the same as that of the firm. Mr. Evarts, Sec. of State, to Mr. Foster, Min. to Mexico, No. 725, Feb. 20, 1880, For. Rels. 1880, 73." Moore, *Digest*, V: 34.

The practice followed by the United States in its consular conventions has not been uniform: in some such agreements the contracting states have stipulated for the inviolability of the consular offices and dwellings; in a larger number they have stipulated for such immunity for the office alone; in still others the matter has not been mentioned; and in a few there has been recognized the right of the local authorities to enter the consulate for certain purposes. This variation in practice would indicate that for some time the Department of State might have been uncertain as to the necessity for the provision; but it is significant that all of the later conventions stipulate for inviolability of the consular office. It would seem that the Department has felt the desirability of protecting the consular business from unexpected interruptions which might occur where the consulate is not regarded as inviolable. But even where inviolability has been secured by treaty, discretion should be used in taking advantage of it. The utilization of the privilege may have a tendency to draw the consul into conflicts with the local authorities which, instead of furthering the good feeling which is so advantageous to the successful conduct of the consular functions, would tend to bring the consul into disfavor with these officials and hamper him in the discharge of his duties. The privilege should never be used to defeat the local justice. Generally, even where inviolability has been accorded to the consulate, there is no reason for its extension to the dwelling of the consul. Such is the view presented with considerable force by the Italian government as a basis for its denunciation in 1877 of the consular convention entered into with the United States in 1868; and the new convention entered into the year following did not contain the provision objected to.[1]

[1] After stating that only the conventions between Italy and the United States and Italy and Belgium carried provisions for the inviolability of

Presumably international law has developed no rule according inviolability of the consulate because the local laws sufficiently protect the offices and homes of persons within its jurisdiction. If this be the case, any violation of these laws resulting in a violation of the consulate affords a just ground for protest on the part of the consul's government. Acts by individuals or by mobs which are the occasion of danger or damage to the consulate are usually protested against, and are usually followed by apologies on the part of the government which has received the consul, and by the apprehension and punishment of the offenders.[1]

the dwelling of the consul but that through the most-favored-nation clause this privilege was extended to the consuls of other states as well, the Italian Minister of Foreign Affairs continued:

> It is not necessary for me to use words to explain to you how such a state of things is in little harmony with the modern principles of international law, which principles have to take into consideration the progress of civilization and of the greatly extended guarantees sanctioned by modern laws for the protection of individual liberty and of the inviolability of domicile, and have then to leave open the way for the common law, reserving the privilege of exemption only to the dwellings of diplomatic agents, the true representatives of foreign sovereignty.
>
> On the other hand, once that the principle is admitted of consular officers being liable to summons before the tribunals of the kingdom, to there answer for responsibilities contracted by them, and, to a certain point, also for offenses charged against them, it does not seem logical that to them should be granted, by means of this exemption, the way of evading for themselves and their effects the execution of the sentence. (*Foreign Relations*, 1878, pp. 462-463.)

The convention of 1868 had stipulated for inviolability of the consular office and dwelling; that of 1878 for inviolability of the consular office only.

[1] The object for which such attacks might be committed is indicated in a statement contained in *Foreign Relations*, 1911, giving the background of the notes relative to Mexican affairs published in that year:

> Attacks upon consulates, insults to the flag, assaults upon the persons of American citizens and destruction of their property were acts calculated to embarrass the Mexican Government, since it could do no less than suppress such demonstrations. These suppressive measures were

While the claim for inviolability in the absence of treaty provision may be taken as without adequate foundation, courtesy would seem to demand a certain amount of respect for the consular premises. A strict compliance with the local law which would involve inconvenience to the consul would not afford a basis for any legal claim against the officers obeying the law; but some such step as notification of the consul in advance, where feasible, that the premises are to be entered for certain purposes in order that he may be sure to be present at the time—or even asking him to fix a time when such an entry would be most convenient to him—would involve no surrender of right on the part of the state and yet would forestall any complications which might otherwise arise.[1] It is this idea which probably actuated the insertion of provisions in some treaties requiring "respect" for the consulate; and it has been inserted into the laws and regulations of a few states.

In addition to the denials of inviolability which accompany the vigorous statements regarding asylum in consulates, there are to be found the following express denials of the alleged right:

*Belgium:* Article 3 of the regulations applying to the Congo limits the right of entry into the consulate in this manner:

> interpreted to the people as clear evidence of the close understanding between Cientifico and Gringo; and such arguments multiplied volunteers for the revolutionary army. (Page 354.)

The files of the Department of State and the pages of *Foreign Relations* contain numerous instances where mobs in Latin American states have outraged American consulates; such actions have been uniformly followed by apologies, efforts to apprehend the offenders, and steps to repair the damage done.

[1] In 1899 the United States protested the invasion of the residence of its deputy consul at Port au Prince, Haiti, on the ground that the proceedings "were not conducted with suitable consideration for Mr. Battiste's official position." Moore, *Digest*, V: 55-57. And see generally, *ibid.*, pp. 48-57.

The authorities can not on any pretext enter the office building if the incumbent is a full consul, subject of the country which nominated him, and not trading. They can, however, do so with the consent of the director of justice, if he has granted asylum to persons threatened with criminal prosecution.

Except in the case of *flagrante delicto,* no search shall be made except in the presence and with the formal decree of the judge.

*Bolivia:* On May 28, 1890 Bolivian police entered the Argentine consulate general at La Paz in search of a refugee, without having given formal notice of their intention to search the consulate and without exhibiting their authority to do so. The Argentine protest was based upon a treaty provision to the benefits of which Argentina was entitled under the most-favored-nation clause; and the Bolivian apology was likewise rested upon this. See Bolivian *Informe,* 1890, *Anexos* 1-5; and Guesalga, *Derecho Diplomático y Consular con los Ultimos Casos de Controversias entre los Estados,* pages 177, 178.

*Esthonia:* " Rooms where consuls are located do not enjoy inviolability. . . ." Instructions issued by Chief Police Administration, contained in a despatch from the legation at Riga, Latvia, to the Secretary of State, on Dec. 7, 1922.

*Guatemala:* The *Apéndice al Reglamento Consular de la República* contains the following:

As a consequence of the preceding paragraph (which asserted that consuls were not public ministers), they (consuls) do not enjoy the immunities which belong to diplomatic ministers, and which are:

. . . (b) Immunity for their place of residence, and therefore exemption from the local jurisdiction with respect to their personal or moveable property. (Paragraph 5.)

*Honduras:* The law on foreign consuls recognizes that a

certain respect is due to the consular office. The extent of any privilege which this respect might confer is not marked out in the act; but it clearly falls short of inviolability. In terms the act states the consular office can not serve to take persons or effects from the local jurisdiction. The language employed is:

> The consular office and dwelling of the consuls, will be equally respected, but it is not intended by this to recognize in them the right of asylum with regard to persons or effects which are endeavoring to withdraw from the action of the authorities. (Article 36.)

When the government of Honduras had reason to believe that the person who occupied the building taken over for the British consular office in Tegucigalpa before the British had taken possession had stored there quantities of arms and ammunition to be used in fostering a revolt, permission to search the building was requested. Pending authorization by the embassy the secretary to the president agreed that the search would not be pushed, as the inviolability of the office had been secured by treaty. Before the authorization arrived, the consulate was searched on November 6, 1911 under a writ issued by the supreme court. A protest was immediately filed.

*Salvador:* Article 38 of the law governing foreign consuls is similar to the Honduranean provision given above

*Spain:* According to the decree of January 1, 1765 "the houses of consuls do not enjoy any immunity" Bursotti, I: 208.

*Venezuela:* Confusion is apparent in the Consular Regulations of 1887 (article 33) and 1905 (article 31) which provide that:

> There being no particular conventions which authorize it, consuls can not claim other privileges than those conceded in

like case by Venezuela to foreign consuls; that is, independence in the exercise of their functions, compatible with the laws in force in the territory in which they exercise them; inviolability of the office. . . .

It is believed that at the time those regulations were issued there was nothing in the laws of Venezuela granting such an inviolability, nor is any record of a practice to that effect apparent. The statement was evidently an error; it was not repeated in the later editions of the Consular Regulations.

### USE OF THE CONSULATE AS AN ASYLUM

The general rule is clear that the consulate may not be used as an asylum. Provisions in consular regulations relative to the display of the national flag frequently state expressly that such a display is never to be taken as conferring upon the consulate the character of an asylum. Similar limitations upon a possible extension of the inviolability of the consular archives sometimes are to be found. In still other regulations specific denials of such a right, independent of any connection with either of the two privileges above stated, are incorporated. And in those documents which purport to list the privileges to be claimed by consuls, the absence of any claim to the use of the consulate as an asylum is uniformly to be noted. No set of instructions to consuls has been found which authorizes these officers to claim a right of asylum for their offices. In specific instances, however, particularly in Latin America, consulates have been used to give asylum to political refugees; and in some of these cases such a use has not been challenged, or if challenged, has been sustained by the consul's government.

The chief reason for the denial of the right so to use the consulate is that this involves a surrender of sovereignty which is seldom granted and is never to be implied. Nevertheless, there is a certain respect to which the consulate is entitled and which is usually accorded; in the matter of the use of the consulate as an asylum it consists of a request to the consul to surrender the person who has taken refuge in the consulate. Wherever practicable, it is desirable in the event of the refusal of the consul to make such surrender, to request his government to instruct him to do so; and this is sometimes done. The refusal of the consul to surrender a person who has taken refuge in the consulate has been made the occasion of the revocation of the exequatur of the consul; and since no reason need be given for such revocation, the right of the offended government to take this action can not be challenged.

The situation with regard to the use of consulates in Latin America as places of asylum is decidedly uncertain. The history of these states has, unfortunately, been one of turbulence and too frequent inability of governments to control the acts of individuals. Under such conditions, from considerations of humanity and justice, political refugees have been permitted to enter consulates to escape mob violence. At times the consular offices have been respected, and the refugees permitted to escape; and the government established by the revolution, or in power despite the revolution, has been willing to let the matter drop. At other times, the consulate has been forcibly entered, and the refugee removed; such action has on some occasions brought a protest from the government whose consulate has been entered, and at other times a disavowal of the action of the consul. From such divergent practices it is impossible to draw a general rule applicable to all cases.[1] So far as the United States is concerned, it is believed that the rule deducible from the

[1] Dr. Alvarez in his book *Le Droit International Américain* surveys a number of cases in which consulates have been used as asylums (pp. 72-82). According to the author the United States has indicated that it will give up all claim to such right if the European states will concur. Until such time each case is to be decided on its merits.

cases is this: where the offender is fleeing from a mob which the local authorities are unable to control, the consul will be upheld if he gives temporary refuge; but where the offender is fleeing from the legally constituted authorities, the consul may not grant refuge. In other words, asylum may be granted to further, but not to thwart, the local justice.[1]

However, at no time has there been any indication by any government that the practice of granting asylum in Latin America was anything but temporary, a practice called into existence by the unsettled conditions in those countries. As soon as conditions warrant, the practice doubtless will be discontinued. But there has been and will continue to be a difference of opinion as to when stability has been permanently established. It seems that the limitation upon state sovereignty involved in the practice is such that it should not be continued any longer than is essential; and that doubts as to stability should be resolved in favor of the territorial sovereign. The possible act of inhumanity to the individual would not be such a disruption of international order as is the impairment of state sovereignty in order to prevent it.[2]

[1] See Hyde, *International Law*, vol. i, pars. 443 and 467 and authorities there cited. The theory seems to be that temporary conditions exist which have impaired the power or disposition of the local authorities to administer justice for the time being. Before a consular officer is justified in granting asylum he should therefore assure himself that such conditions do exist and continue to exist during the period the shelter is granted. That the offense for which the refugee is sought is essentially a political one is not sufficient, at least if such offense is made punishable by the local law; there must be reason to believe that the rights usually accorded accused persons will not be respected in his case.

[2] On the general question see J. B. Moore, *Asylum in Legations and Consulates*, New York, 1892; Robin, "Le droit d'asile politique," *Rev. Gen.*, XV: 572 (1908); and Gilbert, "The practice of asylum in legations and consulates of the United States," *AJIL*, III: 562-595 (1909). An interesting viewpoint in connection with asylum in Latin America is presented in an article by Dr. Jose Leon Suarez on "Las guerras civiles Americanas" in *Revista Diplomática y Consular Argentina* for December, 1915.

Even though no treaty exists to accord inviolability to the consulate, the authorities may not at will invade the consulate on a mere suspicion that perhaps the person whom they are seeking has taken refuge there; unless there is a basis for a reasonable supposition that the consulate is being used to harbor the person sought, the action of the police officers in entering the consulate will afford an occasion for a diplomatic protest.[1]

In addition to those expressions of governmental practice found in the two preceding sections of this chapter, the following may be noted:

*Argentina:* Article 29 of the regulations of 1862 denying any right of asylum was changed by the regulations of 1906, article 62, to read:

> They do not have nor can they pretend to the right of asylum in their houses; these are subject to the civil and criminal jurisdiction of the country in which they are located, lacking, in consequence, the faculty of withdrawing from the investigations of justice the individuals who reside or take refuge in them.

*Bolivia:* In that portion of the consular regulations of 1887 dealing with foreign consuls in Bolivia, article 100 provides that: "The houses of the consuls do not enjoy the privilege of extraterritoriality, and in consequence can not serve as an asylum for offenders who take refuge in them."

*Brazil:* The privilege of asylum is denied to consulates by article 21 of the imperial decree of 1851 in these terms:

> The houses in which consular agents reside do not enjoy the right of affording asylum, nor do they prevent the serving of writs, arrests, or the execution of fiats issued by the justices of the country, due deference being observed as well as the guarantees and formalities established by the laws. (*British and Foreign State Papers*, vol. 42, p. 1316.)

[1] See *infra*, p. 95.

This was simply applying to foreign consuls in the national territory the rule enjoined upon Brazilian consuls abroad under the terms of article 28 of the consular regulations of 1830.

*Chile:* See page 63 *supra.* A portion of article 112 of the regulations of 1915 amplifies the provision cited, as follows:

> In no case can the consular officers exercise in their dwellings or offices the right of asylum, which they do not possess; nor can they impede the investigations of the territorial authorities with respect to individuals who reside or take refuge in these, even though they be Chilean citizens.

In 1859 local police officials in Valparaiso entered the American consulate by mistake, having confused it with the American hospital with which it was connected and to which they were bound for prisoners. After controversy with the consul, the police withdrew without the prisoners. The Chilean government communicated with the American minister and later informed the consul that there was no right of asylum in consulates. Police officials then returned with a request for the surrender of the persons desired. After trying for two hours to induce those individuals to give themselves up, the consul refused to comply with the request. As a result his exequatur was withdrawn. In answer to the American protest, the Chilean government maintained that its action was in accordance with the principles of the United States government, and cited treaty provisions to support the statement. Seijas, *El Derecho Internacional Hispano-Americano,* I: 443-448; also Wharton, *Digest,* I: 676.

*Colombia:* The regulations are similar to those of Chile, page 63 *supra.* *Guía Consular,* page 30; Perez-Sarmiento, *Manual Consular,* page 38.

In consequence of the state of inquietitude and uneasiness in the Republic when the circular of August 5, 1876 over the cessation of the pretended right of asylum of co·isuls, was communicated to the foreign legations, this provision, purely doctrinal and which tends to reestablish the true ideas and principles of international law with reference to consular functions and immunities beginning with the reference to the said right of asylum, which implied exterritoriality of the dwelling of these agents—was improperly interpreted.

The President, who desired to avoid on his part, in such dangerous circumstances, every act which might contribute in the least to increase the discord in the country, resolved that for the time he would yield quietly this incident and not take any new step in the practice of asylum in political buildings, reserving always the principle of law relating to the immunities of consuls.

Calm restored by the reestablishment of peace and assured of its maintenance for many years because of the splendid victory and the unexampled generosity of the victors, the time has come to place in force this declaration, which for exceptional reasons did not go into effect from the time it was given. (Circular quoted in Uribe, *Anales Diplomáticos y Consulares de Colombia*, III: 813-818.)

*Costa Rica:* "The consular dwelling or office can not give asylum to any criminals, even though they be Costa Ricans, nor can the coat of arms or the flag obstruct the speed of citation, commitment, or execution of the justice of the country." Regulations of 1888, article 30.

*Cuba:* The terms of the *Instrucciones Provisionales,* pages 6 and 7, are quite similar to those of article 112 of the Chilean regulations of 1915, *supra.*

*Honduras:* See page 85 *supra* for the provisions of the law on foreign consuls. Consuls of the republic are under instructions similar to those of Costa Rica *supra.* Regulations of 1906, article 35.

*Mexico:* Article 29 of the law of 1859 is applicable to the position of foreign consulates in Mexico:

The consular office and consular dwelling . . . will be equally respected; but it will not be understood from this that there is conceded to them the privilege of asylum with respect to persons or effects which are attempting to withdraw themselves from the authority of Mexican authorities and officers.

The position to be maintained by Mexican consuls abroad was expressed in these terms in article 149 of the regulations of 1911:

Neither the offices nor, much less, the dwellings of the consular agents have the right of asylum, and, therefore, these agents will not oppose in any case investigations which the local authorities desire to make, nor place themselves in opposition to the apprehension of persons who have taken refuge in them.

The regulations of 1923 superseding those of 1911 contain a list of privileges which Mexican consuls may expect to enjoy; nothing is said of a right of asylum under this or any other head.

*Paraguay:* Consuls of the Republic are "forbidden to harbor or conceal any persons, either Paraguayans or foreigners, who are subject to the action of the tribunals of the country." Regulations of 1871, article 37.

*Peru:* The provisions of the regulations of 1888, article 264, and 1897, article 232, bear a close resemblance to those of Chile quoted page 63 *supra*.

*Russia:* "In Kertch I have known the police to enter the yard and force the door of the consulate in pursuit of a British subject, whom I sheltered from injustice, and from unjustifiable persecution." *Reports relative to British Consular Establishments,* II: 89.

"However, his consulate may not serve as a shelter for

persons and objects not belonging to it." Summary of a decree of the Soviet Government published in Moscow *Isvestia* for July 7, 1921.

*South African Republic:* During the period of its existence, the Republic had a provision in its regulations similar to that of the Netherlands quoted page 70 *supra,* Article 4.

*Sweden:* " The inviolability of the consular archives has even in later consular conventions been extended to the office and dwelling of paid consuls, but nevertheless these premises must not under any circumstances be used as places of refuge." *Swedish Consular Ordinance and Instructions,* Rule 78.

*Uruguay:* Article 71 of the regulations of 1906 and article 56 of those of 1917 contain provisions identical with those of article 112 of the Chilean regulations set out on page 63 *supra.* The regulations of 1878, article 40, were to the same effect though in greater detail.

*Venezuela:* See page 74 *supra.* According to a *memoria* presented in 1880:

> . . . there has been modified the so-called right of asylum in legations and consulates, which, however, is undoubtedly retained in certain of these weak Republics; for though they protest against its use, these same ones (presumably the more powerful states) see them obliged to concede it as is said from considerations of humanity and sympathy with the unfortunate. With respect to the houses of consuls it has been suppressed completely by mutual consent and even by internal laws.

*United States:* In 1908 Secretary Root in a statement applying to both legations and consulates instructed the American minister in Haiti that " this Government does not recognize the so-called right of asylum ".[1] While this is

[1] *Foreign Relations,* 1908, 435; Hyde, *International Law,* I: 762. This was interpreted in 1912 to permit the consul at his discretion to give

true, the government has maintained that it is entitled to the same consideration as other nations in this regard; thus when the exequatur of an American consul in Chile was revoked because he had permitted the consulate to be used as an asylum, the United States protested because it seemed that other consuls in Chile had not been penalized for similar action.[1]

By far the greater number of cases in which American consulates have been used as places of asylum have arisen in Latin America. The exceptional situation in those republics has been mentioned above.[2] As stated there, the American rule deducible from the many cases which have arisen seems to be that the consular officer who grants asylum to persons fleeing from mobs will be supported by the Government of the United States; but that the officer who presumes to give refuge to an individual fleeing from the local justice will find himself subject to the censure of his government.

Treaties entered into by the United States have not carried uniform provisions on the subject of this chapter. Though the differences have been slight in the main, seventeen different combinations have resulted from the twenty

temporary refuge "in order to preserve innocent human life." *For. Rels.*, 1912, 925; Hyde, I: 798.

Among the communications denying the right of asylum may be noted those in Wharton, *Digest*, I: 676-678.

But this does not mean that the consulate can be invaded at will on the suspicion that it is being used as an asylum. Hay, Sec. of State, to Mr. Powell, April 25 and Nov. 27, 1899. Moore, *Digest*, V: 55-57.

In 1904 the Department of State was of opinion that an American consul "was perhaps justified" in granting asylum to a political refugee in Santo Domingo. *For. Rels.*, 1904, 286-288. And in 1914 a consul in Haiti was authorized to grant asylum if necessary to save the lives of certain refugees. *Ibid.*, 1914, 385.

[1] June 17, 1859. Wharton, *Digest*, I: 676. This stand was reiterated Nov. 7, 1885. Bayard, Sec. of State, to Mr. Thompson. *Ibid.*, 692.

[2] *Supra*, p. 88.

treaties which make specific provision for this group of privileges. Thus the arms and inscription are usually provided for, in some cases for the office and in others for dwellings as well. Hoisting of the national colors is permitted over offices, or dwellings, or the boat used in the discharge of duties, and over various combinations of these, with an exception sometimes made in cities where a legation is established. Inviolability of the consular office is frequent, with an occasional extension to the dwelling of the consul, though various limitations are placed upon it. Finally the denial of the right to use the office as an asylum is usual, though a few treaties make no definite provision. In the following table an attempt has been made to show briefly the various combinations; and to make the differences more apparent a system of lettering has been used. (A) introduces provisions regarding the arms and inscription, with (1) referring to the office and (2) to the dwelling; (B), the national insignia with (1) the office, (2) the dwelling, (3) the rule in cities which have legations, and (4) the boat used in the consular business; (C) the provision regarding inviolability with (1) the office, and (2) the dwelling; and finally (D) the provisions relative to the use of the consular offices and dwellings for purposes of asylum.

Considered in this light the treaties fall into the following groups:

1. (C1) Full and entire immunity for their chancery; may place over outward door of their house (A) arms of their sovereign, but (D) there is no privilege of asylum for any person or property.

France, CC, 1788: II.

2. (C) Persons and property and their houses inviolate.

Muscat, A&C, 1833: IX (adopted by Zanzibar, AC&N, 1886: II.)

3. "In order that the (B2) dwellings of consuls may be

easily and generally known, for the convenience of those who may have to resort to them," may hoist on them the flag and (A2) place over the door the coat of arms and inscription; (D) not to import a right of asylum or be considered as placing the house or inhabitants beyond the authority of magistrates who may think proper to search and who have that right as with the houses of other inhabitants under the laws. Persons and dwellings subject to laws and authorities where not exempted in the convention—as other inhabitants.

Colombia, CC, 1850: V, VI.

4. (A1, 2) Over door of offices or dwelling-houses, may place arms and inscription; (B1, 2) may hoist flag thereon. (C1, 2) Offices and dwellings inviolable; local authorities may not invade under any pretext; (D) in no case may they be used as an asylum.

France, CC, 1853: II, III.[1]

[1] In 1899 the American consul at Bordeaux, France, on the advice of his physician, established a temporary residence at Archachon, thirty miles distant but within his consular district. Here the consular business was in large part transacted. These premises were entered by a bailiff, over the consul's protest, in search of property to attach under a writ sued out in a case in which the consul was defendant. The entry was protested under the treaty of 1853, and the claim was taken up by the United States. The French government contended that the provision applied only to protect the consular dwelling when in the same city with the consular office, and had been inserted because it might be difficult to make a distinction between them. While the United States did not think that this interpretation was consistent with the language of the provision, it was acquiesced in by the Department of State. *Foreign Relations*, 1900, 429-456.

The court at Limoges on May 12, 1899 handed down a decision to this effect:

"Judged that, under the terms of article 3 of the convention between France and the United States of America, of September 15, 1853, the chancelleries and the consular habitations are inviolable."

"This inviolability, which protects at the same time the office of the consulate and the private domicile of the consul, extends to all the furniture and other property which serve for the personal use of the consul or for that of his house, and which are necessary for him to live with independence and dignity, on the territory of the nation near which he is accredited; consequently one must regard as unattachable the

5. (A1) Arms and inscription on consulates (D) do not confer right of asylum or exempt house or those dwelling therein from prosecution of local justice.

Netherlands, CC (cols.), 1855: IV.

6. (A1, 2) Arms and inscription over offices and dwellings; (B1, 2, 3) may raise flag over offices or dwellings except in capital when there is a legation there. (C1, 2) Consular offices and dwellings inviolable; local authorities may not invade under any pretext; (D) in no case may they be used as places of asylum.

Belgium, CC, 1868: V, VI.

Italy, CC, 1868: V, VI.[1]

7. (A1) Arms and inscription over chief entrance to offices; (B1, 3, 4) hoist flag on consular edifice, except where there is a legation, and over boat employed in port.

Austria-Hungary, CC, 1870: IV.[2]

8. (C1, 2) Consular offices and dwellings inviolable; local authorities can under no pretext invade; (D) in no case may they be used as asylum. In order that (B2) dwellings may be more easily and generally known, may hoist flag and (A2) place over doors the arms and inscription.

Salvador, AC&CP, 1870: XXXV.[3]

9. (C1, 2) Consular offices and dwellings inviolable; local authorities may under no pretext, except in case of pursuit for crime, invade; (D) in no event may they be used as asylum. (A1, 2) Arms and inscription over outer door of offices and dwellings. (B1, 3, 4) May hoist flag on consular edifice except where there is a legation, and on vessel used in port.

German Empire, CC, 1871: IV, V.[4]

equipment which furnishes not only the offices properly so-called of the consulate, but also the dwelling of the consul, and which are in any way the complement of this habitation, in the inviolability of which they participate." (*Pandectes Françaises*, Supplement, vol. ii, 292.)

[1] For an interpretation, see Moore, *Digest*, V: 37.

[2] Applied in the face of a conflicting municipal ordinance. *Ibid.*, V: 58; *Foreign Relations*, 1884, 18, 19.

[3] For an application, see Moore, *Digest*, V: 51.

[4] For an application, see *ibid.*, V: 81, 82.

10. (A1) Arms and inscription over office; (B1, 3) flag over office where no legation. (C1) Consular office inviolable; local authorities may not enter under any pretext; (D) may never serve as place of asylum.

Italy, CC, 1878: V, VI.[1]

11. (A1, 2) Arms and inscription over outer door of office and residence; (B1, 2, 4) flag over office or dwelling and over vessel used in port. (D) In no event may office and dwelling be used as asylum.

Netherlands, CC, 1878: V, VI.

12. (A1) Arms and inscription over outer door of office; (B1, 3, 4) flag on offices, except where legation, and over boat used in port. (C1) Offices inviolable; under no pretext may local authorities invade; (D) in no case may they be used as asylum.

Belgium, CC, 1880: V, VI.
Servia, CC, 1881: V, VI.
Roumania, CC, 1881: V, VI.
Spain, F&GR, 1902: XVII, XVIII.

13. (B1) Flag over offices; (C) offices inviolable, local authorities not to invade under any pretext; (D) not to be used as asylum.

Congo, AC&N, 1891: V.

14. (A1) Arms and inscription over office; (B1, 4) flag over office and boat. (C1) Office inviolable; local authorities may not invade under any pretext; (D) may not be used as asylum.

Greece, CC, 1902: V, VI.

15. (A1) Arms and inscription over office; (B1, 3, 4) flag over office, except where legation, and over boat; (C1) local authorities may not invade under any pretext.

Sweden, CC, 1910: V, VI.

16. Dwelling respected.

Morocco, Convention as to Protection, 1880: VI.

[1] This provision was invoked when the Italian consular agency at Birmingham, Ala., was searched for alcoholic liquors on April 5, 1919. The Department of State requested an investigation and the punishment of the guilty officer.

17. (A1) Arms and inscription over office; (B1, 3, 4) flag over offices, including that in capital, and over boat. (C1) Offices at all times inviolable; under no circumstances to be subjected to invasion by any authorities of any character, nor shall any authorities make any examination of papers or property deposited therein. (D) Offices not be used as asylums.

Germany, FC&CR, 1923: XX.

As the treaty of friendship, commerce and consular rights with Germany is the latest expression of the policy of the United States, it may be well to stress the privileges there granted. The unqualified statement regarding the arms and inscription considered in the light of their character clearly shows that the right to attach these is the right to keep them there permanently. It is to be noted that this treaty extends the right to fly the flag to consulates located in the capital of the country; the restriction in this regard to be found in some of the earlier treaties is illogical. The present provision incorporates the better rule. Nothing is said of the purpose for which the flag may be displayed nor of the times at which such display may be made. If the reasoning of the Knox instructions [1] be applied, it would seem that the interpretation of the provision is that the flag may be flown at all times. It is clear that the provision is open to that interpretation.

In line with the correspondence relative to the denunciation of the Italian treaty of 1868 [2] inviolability is extended only to the consular office and not to the consular dwelling. It may be recalled that the French interpretation of the consular convention of 1853 was that inviolability was granted to the consular dwelling in order better to secure that of the consular office.[3] With the background of the corre-

[1] *Supra*, p. 78.

[2] *Supra*, p. 82.

[3] *Supra*, p. 97.

spondence in these two cases, it is probable that the present treaty marks a definite relinquishment of attempts to secure inviolability for the consular dwelling. Inviolability of the office is complete; under the provisions of this treaty there can be no interruption of the consular business due to an invasion of the consular office for any purpose. Naturally enough, the inviolability of the office extends to the property within it. There is no reason to believe that the interpretation of this provision will differ from that of the treaty of 1853 with France, i. e. that should the consul attempt to use the office to protect property which does not properly belong there, his government will instruct him to surrender such property after due notice to the government from whose jurisdiction the consul is endeavoring to withdraw the property.[1]

The consular office may not be used as a place of asylum. Here again it is to be noted that this provision is not a limitation upon the inviolability of the consulate. Use of the consulate as an asylum would be a violation of the treaty; but it would not afford any ground for an invasion of the consulate by the local authorities.

[1] *Supra*, p. 37.

## CHAPTER IV

### Exemption from Taxation

There is no rule of international law under which consuls may claim exemption from taxation. Such a statement standing alone, however, would come far from indicating the actual position of the consular officer. Theorists writing on the subject of consular privileges have questioned the place of exemption from taxation among those privileges, on the ground that such an exemption is not essential to the conduct of the consular business. The trend has been quite different: exemption from taxation, hardly granted at first, is now unquestioned. Consular regulations regularly state that, as a matter of local legislation and custom, consuls are accorded exemption from certain types of taxation, whereas the earlier regulations were silent upon the subject. The custom of exempting consuls from taxation is becoming firmly fixed; and the list of taxes from which those officers are to be exempt tends to become increasingly greater.

Generalizations are hard to make and if made would be inaccurate, because of the differences in the systems of taxation used by the various states of the world. Practically the only statement which can be made with strict accuracy is that consuls are generally exempt from some forms of taxation; a determination of the exemption to which a particular consul is entitled must await a study of the laws of the state in which he is situated. Such a study is beyond the scope of the present work, though in the pages following some indication will be given of the variety of the exemptions which have at times been accorded. That states find the exemption from taxation of some importance is indicated by the increasing frequency with which taxation provisions are being inserted in treaties. Unfortunately for a logical treatment of the subject, these provisions have not been uniform; though by a method of trial and error it seems that there is an approach to a norm. A comprehensive statement of exemption carried in a few conventions and extended by the most-favored-nation clause would do much toward bringing uniformity in the place of the present variety; but such a provision is not yet in sight.

The present chapter will take up general statements together with examples of exemption from miscellaneous taxes, then more particularly customs duties and income taxes—the exemptions exciting the most interest today. The treatment is not designed to be exhaustive; rather it considers merely typical instances of exemption.

*Argentina:* Exemption from a tax on telegraph messages sent by consuls of Brazil, Chile, and Bolivia to their colleagues was accorded by a decree of February 23, 1918. *Memoria del Ministerio de Relaciones Esteriores,* 1917-1918, p. 203.

*Austria-Hungary:* In 1831 the government of Trieste ruled that consuls "are held as ordinary individuals to the discharge of taxes, and of all other general contributions prescribed by law". Bursotti, *Guide des Agents Consulaires.*

*Belgium:* In the first part of the nineteenth century there was recognized an exemption from direct and personal taxes, both state and local, on the basis of reciprocity. Royal decree summarized in a note from Henri G. T. Mali to Forsyth, Sec. of State, May 19, 1838; Belgium, Notes, I. The British consul at Antwerp on January 4, 1872 reported exemption from "certain personal taxes" but not from those on real property and in no case from indirect taxes of any description. *Reports relative to British Consular Establishments,* I: 22.

A decree of Jan. 1, 1856 is to the following effect: " Consuls who are foreigners and who aside from their consular functions do not engage in commerce or in any profession whatever, will be exempt: 1. From the personal tax for the benefit of the state, of the province, of the communes. . . . " *British State Papers,* 47: 991.

Likewise consuls of career in the Congo were held to be exempt from personal taxation.

*Bolivia:* Article 99 of the *Reglamento Consular* of 1887, under the heading " Foreign Consuls Resident in Bolivia " provides for their exemption from " personal tributes and taxes, but not from duties on effects for use and consumption, as customs duties, *porte de cartes* and others, conformably to the laws in force ".

*Brazil:* In 1871 and 1872 British consuls in Brazil reported as follows: Rio Grande do Sul, exemption from local taxes; Pernambuco, " the consul pays taxes and imposts, even duties upon the stationery required for the use of the office and declared to be such "—but exempt from tax on consular office; Santos, exemption from all taxes; Rio de Janeiro, exemption from direct taxes. *Reports relative to British Consular Establishments,* IV: 130, 112, 137, 143.

*Canada:* When in 1913 the city council of Victoriaville imposed a tenant's tax upon the American consular agent in that city, the latter protested claiming that he was entitled to an exemption. He was advised by the consul at Quebec to pay the tax if his protest were not heeded. That officer informed the consular agent that while no tax of any kind had been imposed upon consuls at Quebec, consular agents at Victoriaville had regularly paid a small tenant's tax. The Secretary of State approved the reply of the consul on November 18, 1913.

*Denmark:* " Salaried consuls are, as a rule exempt from every personal onus, as well as from personal dues or taxes. . . . " *Consular Instructions,* par. 86.

*France:* Lehr quotes from a circular letter of the director of direct taxes under the date of January 9, 1875 to the effect that " it is advisable to exempt from personal taxes on movables and the doors and windows, those consuls of foreign nations, in which French consuls enjoy an equal privilege either by virtue of conventions of this nature or through application of the principle of reciprocity. According to information furnished by the Minister of Foreign Affairs, this immunity is applicable to the consuls of every country except England; but this immunity need be accorded at all times only to those who are subjects of the state which names them and solely by reason of their official residence." *Manuel,* sec. 1277. Bertheau, *Dictionnaire Général de Droit et de Jurisprudence,* Vol. 4, p. 397 states that the exemption on doors and windows applies only to the official residence.

The British consul at Marseilles reported that he was the only consul in the city compelled to pay all the local taxes and rates. " As they (French consuls in England) are called upon to pay all the local taxes wherever they may reside in England, this consul is called upon to pay all the French Government and local taxes and rates." *Reports relative to British Consular Establishments,* I: 303, 304. So of the British consul in Algiers, *Ibid.,* I: 50; and with regard to the consular dwelling, that in Cherbourg, *Ibid.,* I: 111. However, the British consul at Bordeaux reported exemption from the house tax on Dec. 29, 1871, *Ibid.,* I: 74; that at Boulogne, exemption from all personal taxes, *Ibid.,* I: 63; and that at Havre, from all direct or personal taxes, *Ibid.,* I: 124.

According to Volume 21 of the *Répertoire des Pandectes*

*Françaises,* p. 379, nos. 110-121, there is exemption from direct personal and sumptuary taxes on the basis of reciprocity, but no exemption from real property taxes, customs duties, and income taxes.

*Germany:* Bursotti, Vol. II, p. 515 contains a summary of privileges granted to foreign consuls in Prussia as indicated by letters from consuls resident there. Exemption from all direct and personal taxes is included.

On May 31, 1923 the Hamburg-American Line, lessors of the building occupied by the American consul general in Hamburg, served notice that a *Grundsteur* or ground tax had been levied to be paid by the tenant to the owner in the amount of 7.20 per cent of the rent paid. The consul general took the matter up with the *Senatskommission* for Foreign Affairs in Hamburg, which ruled that the consul general must pay the tax. The rental law passed by the imperial government had specifically exempted diplomatic and consular premises from its operation. The present law was one of the State of Hamburg. The consul general was also informed that the levy was not really a tax but a *Zuschlag* or additional payment, in this case additional rent. The consul noted, however, that the proceeds were to go into a fund derived from taxation. Having a contract with the Hamburg-American Line for the payment of a fixed rental, the consul general determined to stand on the contract. The matter was finally settled by the act of the steamship company in indicating that the matter would be dropped; presumably the additional rent was paid by the company.

*Great Britain:* Bursotti quotes from a letter received from a foreign consul in London: " You have seen that as for *law* none of these (consular exemptions from taxation) exist; as for *fact* I owe it to justice to say that I have not been subjected up to the present to taxes to which I would have been subject as a simple stranger. I have a horse, a servant and a hunting dog, and I have not been called upon to pay the tax to which I was liable under these three heads." Vol. II, p. 152.

Fourteen American consular officers in the United Kingdom were paying rates and taxes to an amount totalling almost 1,000 pounds in 1921 according to a despatch from the consul general at London on March 3, 1921. See also *France, supra.*

*Guatemala:* Impelled to that decision by a request for reciprocity, the government of the Republic agreed to allow exemption from direct taxes, especially municipal, to all German and Spanish diplomats and consuls residing in the Republic of Guatemala. *Diario Oficial,* Sept. 6, 1923.

*Haiti:* Exemption from all public and municipal contributions which are considered as of a personal nature is granted to all consular officers residing in Haiti on the basis of reciprocity. Law of 1912, Art. 24.

*Honduras:* " They are exempt from every tax or impost purely personal, ordinary or extraordinary, of whatever class." *Ley sobre Misiones Consulares Extranjeras,* Art. 41, sec. 1.

*Italy:* By usage the office of the British consul at Turin was exempt from tax on the rent paid, according to a report of the British consular officer in that city. *Reports relative to British Consular Establishments,* II: 221.

While the requests for the exemption from the payment of the local tax on bicycles, hunting dogs, and guns requested by the American consul at Catania was denied on October 26, 1916 because similar treatment was not accorded Italian consuls in the United States, the minister of foreign affairs stated that " representatives and agents of foreign powers in Italy are exempted from the payment of such local taxes provided that reciprocal treatment shall be accorded to similar representatives of the Italian government on duty in the respective countries of such foreign representatives in Italy. For these same reasons the two automobiles of the American consul in Naples . . . can not be exempted from the payment of a local tax on motor cars."

On December 12, 1921 the consul general at Genoa notified the Secretary of State that exemption from certain luxury taxes established by Article VII of the royal decree of Feb. 27, 1920, No. 167, had been granted to career consular officers in December.

*Mexico:* The law of 1859, Art XVIII, section 5, grants exemption from all purely personal taxes and imposts. Section 4 provides for exemption from all direct real taxes except such as are payable on account of ownership or occupancy of real property.

The American consul general in Mexico City reported on October 12, 1911 that the federal district tax on bicycles amounting to one dollar per month had been remitted on the consulate's bicycle.

The Regulations of 1923 recognize that an exemption from direct taxes may sometimes be claimed on the basis of local legislation and custom, but not as a rule of international law. Art. 55A.

*Netherlands:* The British consul at Amsterdam reported on Dec. 28, 1871 that consuls in that city were exempt from all direct taxes. *Reports relative to British Consular Establishments,* II: 9.

By a decree of June 25, 1885 foreign consuls in the Netherlands are exempted from " local income-tax and other local direct taxation, levied in their principal domicile or other place of residence " on the basis of reciprocity. *Netherlands Consular Instructions,* 1902, p. 38.

*Norway:* Although in 1920 the American consul general at Christiania paid the customary five kroner fee for passport visa while crossing the border between Norway and Sweden, the Norwegian Foreign Office stated that had the consul general sent the passport in to the Foreign Office for visa, such fee would not have been charged.

*Peru:* " Essentially personal " taxes are the only ones from which consular officers may claim to be exempted. *Reglamento sobre admision de cónsules estranjeros* in *Guía Peruanos,* I: 503; see also *Guía,* I: 500.

*Russia:* " The consuls are exempted from requisitions either personal or in kind of (*sic*) State or local." Summary of decree of Soviet Government published in Moscow, *Izvestia* for July 7, 1921.

*Salvador:* The law governing foreign consular missions provides in section 4, article 43, that consular officers " are exempted from all taxes and imposts purely personal, ordinary or extraordinary, of whatever class."

*Spain:* British consuls at Barcelona and in the Philippines reported exemption from taxation in 1871; those in the Canary Islands and in Porto Rico, exemption from direct taxes. *Reports relative to British Consular Establishments,* II: 160, 210, 190, 218.

The decree of Jan. 1, 1765 issued by Charles III to define the position of foreign consuls in Spain exempted them from " communal and personal charges ". Bursotti, I: 208.

*Uruguay:* Under a decree of the ministry for foreign affairs, dated February 4, 1911, consular offices are exempted from taxation only when in the same building with the legation.

Uruguayan consuls abroad are forbidden to treat with the local authorities regarding exemption from municipal taxes or charges except where such right has been expressly established by convention.

*United States:* While as a matter of international comity ambassadors accredited to the United States were exempt from the tax on telegraph, telephone, cable, and radio messages imposed by the Internal Revenue Acts of 1918 and 1921, the Department of the Treasury notified the Secretary of State on May 6, 1922 that such exemption was not extended to consuls.

"A consul is, however, under public law, subject to the payment of taxes and municipal imposts and duties on his property in the country or on his trade." Consular Regulations, 1881, sec. 77; 1888, sec. 50; 1896, sec. 73.

"Sometimes, as a matter of courtesy, and not of right, they are exempted from the payment of a personal tax, but of no other taxes, and more rarely from payment of duties at custom houses on their furniture and baggage." *Ibid.*, 1868, sec. 10.

The British consul in New York on Dec. 18, 1871 escaped payment of federal and municipal taxes assessed against him by showing that United States consuls in the British dominions were exempt from personal taxation. *Reports relative to British Consular Establishments,* IV: 54. That at San Francisco reported an exemption from taxation on furniture, *Ibid.,* IV: 80; that at Mobile, from all taxation of personal property, *Ibid.,* IV: 36; that at Boston, from personal taxation, *Ibid.,* IV: 10; that at Portland, Me., from personal and local taxation, *Ibid.,* IV: 73.

The United States has entered into forty-one treaties to secure for its consuls exemption from taxation. Not all of the treaties have the same specifications; quite the contrary, for at least thirteen distinct types of provisions are ascertainable, and an exemption accorded in one treaty is sometimes specifically refused in another. No logical reason for this, either the dates of the treaties or the standing of the contracting states, is apparent. The provisions are that consuls shall be exempt:

1. From all duties, taxes, impositions, and charges except on

real or personal property of which consuls may be proprietors or in possession.

France, CC, 1788: II.

2. From all taxes, imposts, and contributions except those which they shall be obliged to pay on account of commerce, or their property, to which citizens and inhabitants, native and foreign, of the country in which they reside are subject.

Colombia, AC&N, 1824: XXVIII.
Central America, PAC&N, 1825: XXX.
Denmark, FC&N, 1826: X.
Brazil, AC&N, 1828: XXX.
Chile, PAC&N, 1832: XXVIII.
Venezuela, PAC&N, 1836: XXXI.
Peru-Bolivia, PFC&N, 1836: XXVII.
Ecuador, PFN&C, 1839: XXXI.
Colombia, PFN&C, 1846: XXXII.
Guatemala, PFC&N, 1849: XXX.
Salvador, AC&N, 1850: XXXII.
Peru, PFC&N, 1851: XXXVI.
FC&N, 1870: XXXIII.
FC&N, 1887: XXXI.
Bolivia, PFC&N, 1858: XXXIII.
Haiti, ACN&E, 1864: XXXV.

3. From all taxes, imposts, and contributions levied especially on them, except such as may be due because of commerce or ownership of property.

Mexico, AC&N, 1831: XXIX.

4. From all taxation, federal, state, or municipal unless they own property or engage in business in the state where they reside.

Italy, CC, 1868: III.
Belgium, CC, 1868: III.
Spain, F&GR, 1902: XV.[1]

5. From all direct and personal taxation, whether federal,

[1] The Assistant Secretary of the Treasury notified the Secretary of State on April 7, 1923 that Spanish consuls could claim exemption from a war tax on telegrams by virtue of this provision.

state, or municipal, unless they own property or engage in business in the state where they reside.

France, CC, 1853: II.

Austria-Hungary, CC, 1870: II.[1]

6. From all direct or personal or sumptuary taxes, whether federal, state, or municipal, unless they own property or engage in business in the state where they reside.

Germany, CC, 1871: III.

7. From all national, state, or municipal taxes in the nature of capitation taxes or in respect to property, unless such taxes become due on account of possession of real estate or for interest on capital invested in the state where they reside.

Italy, CC, 1878: III.[2]

8. From all direct taxes, national, state, or municipal in the nature of capitation taxes or in respect to property unless such taxes become due on account of possession of real estate or for interest on capital invested in the state where they reside.

Belgium, CC, 1880: III.

Servia, CC, 1881: III.

Roumania, CC, 1881: III.

Greece, CC, 1902: III.

To the exceptions from the exemption is added pensions of a public or private nature enjoyed from the country where the consul is located, in

Sweden, CC, 1910: III.[3]

[1] The provision in the Austrian convention "refers to all kinds of assessments, forced loans, income and capitation taxes, and other charges levied by the general or local government upon the individual, distinct from property taxes or duties by reason of transactions in which he may engage in the place of his residence. It does not refer to customs duties upon importations collected by the general government, nor to municipal duties on articles of consumption, commonly called *octroi* duties, nor to excise taxes, stamp charges, and the like." Moore, *Digest*, V: 90 summarizing an interpretation by Secretary of State Bayard in 1885. See also *ibid.*, V: 88.

[2] This provision is applicable to Portugal under the treaty of 1840 according to an interpretation given in 1898. Moore, *Digest*, V: 88.

[3] The Assistant Secretary of the Treasury notified the Secretary of State on April 7, 1923 that a Swedish consul could not claim exemption from the war tax on telegrams under this provision.

9. From tax on their official income.

Germany, CC, 1871: III.[1]

10. From all personal taxation and from all public or municipal taxes of a personal character, the exemption never to extend to custom-house duties or other taxes, whether indirect or real.

Netherlands, CC (cols.), 1855: XIII.

11. From all taxes, national, state, provincial, and municipal, except those levied on account of possession or ownership of immovable property in, or income derived from property of any kind situated or belonging within, the state where they exercise their functions; from payment of taxes on official salary, fees, or wages; from duties on official supplies, and on baggage and other personal supplies at entry of consul or imported at any time during his incumbency.

Germany, FC&CR, 1923: XIX, XXVII.

12. From contributions personal and extraordinary.

Colombia, CC, 1850: V.
Salvador, AC&CP, 1870: XXXV.

13. From tariff duties.

Algiers, P&A, 1795, 1815, 1816: XXI.
Tunis, AC&N, 1797: XVII.
Egypt, 1884: X.

The Moroccan convention as to protection contains a peculiar provision to the effect that consuls shall be subject to no duties, imposts, or taxes except the agricultural tax and the gate-tax on beasts of burden.

[1] This provision was interpreted in 1901 in connection with the German insurance law. By the terms of that law, the employer was compelled to defray a certain part of the expense of insuring each of his employees. In nearly every case the American consuls submitted to this provision; but in 1901 the American consul at Breslau claimed that he could not be compelled to pay. The Department of State concurred in this claim but advised the consul voluntarily to submit to the law, thus following the example of his colleagues and giving to the employees the benefit of the measure. The Department observed that he could undoubtedly so arrange that the servants should bear the payment of the quota of the contribution which he was asked to pay. Hill, Acting Sec. of State, to Mr. White, April 30, 1901. Moore, *Digest,* V: 88.

The fact that there has been such a wide variation in the taxation provisions of treaties makes all the more significant the latest expression of this privilege—that in the treaty of friendship, commerce and consular rights with Germany. There the privileges granted extend only to those consular officers (including employees in a consulate) who are nationals of the state by which they are appointed and who are engaged in no private occupation for gain within the state in which they exercise their functions. The general grant is of an exemption from all personal or property taxes levied by any of the units of government. To this general grant there are two exceptions: a consul owning or possessing immovable property in the state in which he is functioning is subject to taxes levied on account of such ownership or possession; and a consul who receives an income from property of any kind situated in or belonging within such a state is subject to the payment of a tax upon that income. Barring these very important exceptions the exemption from personal and property taxes is complete.

Income tax exemption, in so far as it relates to salary, fees, and wages, is specifically provided.[1] Only one earlier treaty, the consular convention of 1871 with Germany, had specifically mentioned an income tax. The income tax law of the United States has been interpreted so as not to require the payment of a tax upon the consular salary when the consul is a national of the state appointing him and that state accords a like favor to American consuls.[2] The Government of the United States has steadily sought to secure for its consuls an exemption from the payment of a tax upon their official income and in some instances has succeeded without a treaty, notably in the case of Canada.[3]

[1] See *infra,* pp. 126-134.

[2] See *infra,* p. 132.

[3] See *infra,* p. 128.

In 1909 an attempt was made to get the British Government to extend its exemption from tax on the official income to cover income derived from property located outside of the United Kingdom; but the extension was refused.[1] The present treaty incorporates what must be taken as the policy of the United States where reciprocity can be secured. The official salary is to be exempt from taxation. Income from property of any kind situated or belonging within the territory of the state in which the consul is functioning may be taxed. Income from sources outside of the state in which the consul is resident is not directly mentioned; but it comes within the scope of the general exemption granted and may not be taxed. It is to be noted that the exemption from the tax on the official income is granted to all consular officers and employees, nationals of the appointing state; while all other tax exemptions may be claimed only by consular officers and employees who in addition to being nationals are not engaged in any private occupation for gain within the state in which they function.

The matter of duties charged upon the entry of official supplies and of the consul's personal effects has been studied by the Department of State upon several occasions.[2] Here again treaty provisions have had to be interpreted and varying provisions have forced a practice differing with the state involved. The present treaty incorporates what seems to be the policy fostered by the United States in every case where reciprocity can be secured. Furniture, equipment, and supplies for official use are to be admitted free without regard to the individual consul to whom they are consigned. Baggage and other personal property of consuls nationals of the state appointing and engaged in no private occupation for gain in the territories of the state to which they are

[1] See *infra,* p. 128.

[2] See *infra,* pp. 122-126.

accredited, likewise is to be accorded free entry. The statement to the effect that the privilege of free entry is to be accorded whether the baggage and personal property arrives with the consul or is imported at any time during his incumbency is novel among American treaty provisions, though it is understood that such a liberal practice has been introduced recently as a matter of reciprocity.

### CUSTOMS DUTIES

The practice of exempting consuls from the payment of certain customs duties is sufficiently widespread to call for separate treatment. Yet it is not so uniform as to permit the statement of a general rule. Here as in the whole field of taxation, no rule of law guarantees the exemption. Treaties, and in their absence varying practices, govern. A few states refuse to admit any exception in favor of tariff exemptions; most states permit some exemptions, but their exact scope varies. Thus while several states restrict the privilege to stationery, others extend it to all official supplies, and still others add personal effects brought in upon arrival. The key note of most of the exemptions is reciprocity within the limits set out in laws, executive ordinances, or customs regulations. The practice of various states may be indicated as follows:

*Argentina:* A circular to the diplomatic body dated August 7, 1907 placed furniture and equipment on the free list on the basis of strict reciprocity. *Anuario,* 1908. In 1914 the list comprised:

(1) Furniture for houses and offices, carriages, motorcars, motorcycles, and bicycles privately owned.

(2) Plate, so long as the pieces are stamped with the monogram, initial, or arms of the owner.

(3) Body linen and wearing apparel, bed and table linen, of which new articles must be marked.

(4) Scientific instruments and accessories of the consular profession.

(5) Pictures, maps, and objects of art of which only one example of each subject is brought in. (*British and Foreign State Papers*, vol. 107, p. 576.)

*Bolivia:* Article 99 of the *Reglamento Consular* of 1887, under the heading " Foreign Consuls Resident in Bolivia ", provides for their exemption from " personal tributes and taxes, but not from duties on effects for use and consumption, as customs duties, *porte de cartes* and others, conformably to the laws in force ".

*Brazil:* The British consul at Pernambuco reported in 1872 that " the consul pays taxes on imports, even duties upon stationery required for the use of the office and declared to be such ". *Reports relative to British Consular Establishments,* vol. II: 112.

In reporting the fact that catalogues entering that country were dutiable, the American consul general at Rio de Janeiro wrote on Sept. 17, 1920 that " Consulates are allowed no exemptions, as that privilege is accorded only to Embassies and Legations ".

*British Colonies*

*Bermuda:* The preamble of an act of October 19, 1911 granting exemption from import duties on the basis of reciprocity reads: " Whereas His Majesty's Government are desirous that in the case of foreign countries which accord substantial privileges to His Majesty's diplomatic and consular officers abroad, similar treatment should be accorded throughout His Majesty's Dominions to the consular representatives of such foreign countries. . . ." *British and Foreign State Papers,* vol. 104, p. 322.

*British Honduras:* On September 28, 1910 an act was passed authorizing the governor to designate states whose consuls should be entitled to receive free of duty official supplies for the use of the consulate, and upon the first arrival of the consul such other articles, goods, and effects as the governor might designate. *Ibid.*, p. 329.

*Gambia:* The act of May 12, 1910 is similar to the above mentioned act of British Honduras. *Ibid.*, p. 451.

*St. Vincent:* An order in council of November 26, 1909 under an Act of 1893 exempts "goods in common official use" from the payment of duty, when sent in to consuls of certain named countries—chosen presumably on a basis of reciprocity. *Ibid.*, p. 553.

*Trinidad:* The customs ordinance of 1920 exempts from duty "articles for the official use of any foreign consulate or the luggage and personal effects of the consular representative of any foreign country, or his family, or suite, if such consular representative is not engaged in any other business or profession in this Colony, provided that a similar privilege is accorded by such foreign country to the British consulate therein". American consul to Secretary of State, Nov. 16, 1920.

*Canada:* There is no exemption on merchandise imported by consuls. Consul, Fort William, to Secretary of State, Jan. 26, 1921.

*Chile:* "I have been charged custom duties on practically everything but personal baggage." Consul, Iquique, to Secretary of State, Dec. 14, 1920. See also post report, Oct. 27, 1920. But on June 17, 1921, the consul at Concepcion reported that the Chilean government granted free entry of supplies destined solely for the use of the consular office.

*China:* On April 2, 1921 the consul at Shanghai reported that he had been compelled to pay customs duties on silverware for "personal and official use", and on May 18 of the same year on an automobile bought in the United States for his personal use.

*Colombia:* The collector of customs charged duties on supplies, including the shield and typewriter, for the vice consulate at Buenaventura, August 19, 1922.

*Cuba:* On page 19 of the *Compilación de Decretos del Sr. Presidente y de Circulares y Consulatas del Departmento Referentes al Servicio Diplomático y Consular* notice is given of an agreement reached between the United States and Cuba permitting reciprocally the free entry of equipment sent directly and officially by either state to its consuls in the other; this indicates that the Cuban practice is one of reciprocal free entry of official supplies.

*Ecuador:* " His (Minister for Foreign Affairs) proposition is substantially stated in the following three heads:

" 1. The Government of Ecuador desires to continue to admit free of duty official supplies for American consuls and consular agencies.

" 2. The laws of Ecuador do not authorize such free entry.

" 3. The Minister suggests that all shipments of consular supplies to American Consulates or Agencies in Ecuador be billed and addressed to ' American Legation, care American Consulate (or Consular Agency), Bahía dé Caráquez (or other location) ', and that if this be done free entry will be granted without any embarrassment to the Government of Ecuador."

This suggestion outlined in a despatch from the American minister at Quito to the Secretary of State on June 6, 1921 is based upon reciprocity in the admission of supplies for Ecuadorean consuls in the United States. In reply the Department indicated that small quantities of consular supplies would be enclosed in the consular pouch, larger quantities addressed as above.

*Guatemala:* " According to Guatemalan law, consuls are not entitled to free entry of their personal supplies into this Republic, and in the past it has been even necessary to secure special permission in order to obtain free entry for official supplies, and samples of merchandise, sent to the Consulate." Practice had varied with the consul, one requesting and securing free entry for all three types of shipments, another paying duty on commercial samples. Consul, Guatemala City, to Secretary of State, Sept. 14, 1920. See also Saravia, *Derecho Patrio,* for paragraph 5c of the *Apéndice al Reglamento Consular de la República.*

*Honduras:* Official supplies are admitted free of duties and imposts, and personal effects are likewise free upon reciprocity granted. *Ley sobre Misiones Consulares Extranjeras,* Art. 41, sec. 5, and Art. 43.

*Italy:* " . . . the Embassy at Rome has advised me that the Ministry of Foreign Affairs has, by virtue of Article 8 of the 'Instructions Preliminary to the Tariff', refused the Embassy its good offices in securing exemptions from customs duties for shipments of office furniture consigned to American consuls in Italy.

"The Italian authorities hold that office furniture is not included under 'stationery supplies' and is therefore not exempted from import duty." A safe sent to the consul general was held until customs duties were paid. Consul general, Genoa, to Secretary of State, Nov. 10, 1921. For a discussion of the question in 1887 see *Foreign Relations,* 1887, p. 633 *et seq.*

*Japan:* There is no exemption from import duties on articles for the consul's personal use. Letter from Japanese consul general at San Francisco, March 24, 1924.

*Mexico:* Articles for the consul's personal use are exempt from duty upon the consul's first entrance into the Republic, on the basis of reciprocity. Likewise a decree of Sept. 11, 1901 exempts from duties shields, flags, seals, and writing materials destined for foreign legations and consular offices when sent by the respective department of state. *Guía*

*Diplomática y Consular,* p. 227. The Regulations of 1923 deny to exemption from customs duties any basis in international law, but state that such exemption is to be claimed in certain countries in accordance with local legislation or custom. Art. 55A.

*Peru:* The only exemption is on official emblems, books, and stamped paper for use in the consulate. Garcia Salazar y Linch, *Guía Práctica para los Diplomáticos y Cónsules Peruanos,* I: 287. In 1871 the British consul at Callao reported that he had been compelled to pay duty on his furniture and upon worn clothing. *Reports relative to British Consular Establishments,* IV: 176.

*Russia:* Under the old regime items sent under official seal and marked *expédition officielle* were not subjected to inspection or to payment of duty. *British and Foreign State Papers* 101: 581, June 10, 1907. So, too, the Russian consul general at Seattle, appointed under the empire, indicated on April 3, 1924 that goods for personal use were granted free entry upon the arrival of the consul and were, thereafter, treated according to principles of reciprocity.

In 1871 the English consul general at Odessa reported that his privileges were confined to receiving books for private use free of duty. *Reports relative to British Consular Establishments,* II: 99.

*Salvador:* "Goods for official and for personal use are admitted upon the principle of reciprocity." *Ley sobre Misiones Consulares Extranjeras,* Art. 44.

*Switzerland:* Duty is charged upon all official supplies save stationery. Consul, Berne, to Secretary of State, Sept. 17, 1920. "For the information of the Department, I beg to state that the goods mentioned in article 40 (of the regulations for the execution of the customs laws) above referred to are: Official signs, flags, blank forms, headed envelopes and headed writing paper. No other official supplies such as pencils, pens, rulers, scissors, rubbers, etc., and no office furniture are mentioned in said article." Chargé to Secretary of State, April 12, 1921. The American practice of sending articles destined for consulates to the legation brought forth a protest from the Swiss government on May 23, 1922.

*Venezuela:* The American consul at Puerto Cabello, reported on Jan. 28, 1922 that he had been granted free entry of personal baggage and household goods upon arrival and of official supplies, though all other articles were dutiable.

"I have had ready for some time a general requisition for a year's supply of everything the office is likely to need and it will go forward in the near future. I am endeavoring to get the local collector of customs to give me in writing over his signature a proper description of these supplies, hoping thereby to be able to avoid the heavy fines which has (*sic*) been regularly assessed against official supplies during the past 18 months.

"The customs still have the supplies which were asked for by special and urgent requisition last November 30. . . . They have asked me to give them a bond for their release, but this I feel I must decline to do." Consul, Maracaibo, to Secretary of State, Feb. 17, 1922.

The Venezuelan consul at New Orleans thus describes the practice of his country: "With respect to the entry of personal effects, the customs law establishes exemption solely for diplomatic officers, moreover courtesy and custom direct that the equipment which the consuls bring in be not examined in the customhouse; later entries are subject to the legal duties."

*United States:* The practice of the United States has not been uniform; but today free entry is accorded all official supplies, and in addition baggage and other effects of the consul on the basis of reciprocity. In view of the actions of other states, this is a liberal position. That it represents the Department of State's idea of what should be the general rule is indicated by permission granted to the American consul at Melbourne to join the other members of the consular corps in an effort "to obtain free entry of personal importations as courtesy and official supplies under reciprocity". Telegram, August 20, 1921.

The variations in the practice of the United States are shown in the following positions taken on the dates given:

*1868:* No authorization had been granted to the Treasury Department to exempt consuls from customs duties. *Consular Regulations,* sec. 10.

*1869:* No immunities had as yet been granted by law, but informally official supplies, particularly blanks and stationery had been granted free entry when a similar privilege had been granted consuls of the United States. J. C. B. Davis, Acting Sec. of State, to Baron Lederer, Aug. 21, 1869.

*1873:* New York collector of customs reported that it was the office practice to collect duty on all dutiable articles sent for use of consuls. *Foreign Relations,* 1873, p. 1380.

*1881:* "It is customary for this Government to admit free of duties and charges at its custom-houses all articles for the official use of the consular officers of foreign states, when similar privileges are granted to its officers. If these privileges are refused in any instance, the refusal should be reported to the Department of State for such proceedings as may be deemed proper." *Consular Regulations,* 1881, sec. 421.

*1884:* General privilege of free entry is denied consuls (art. 366), though free entry is granted for official articles sent directly by a foreign government to its consular officers (art. 367). *Customs Regulations,* 1884.

*1888:* New York customs officials are holding flag, seal, and necessary documents consigned by the Belgian Government to its consular agent in Los Angeles for payment of duties. Thre. de Bounder de Melsbroeck to Bayard, Sec. of State, March 27, 1888.

*1889:* "Under the law now in force the personal effects owned abroad by such (foreign) consuls and also such household effects as were owned and used abroad for not less than one year, are entitled to exemption from duty. Such articles as are required by them for official use are also admitted to free entry, but an examination of the records shows that the Department has always refused to allow them the privilege of free importation.

"The general regulations of 1857 prescribe that the privilege of free entry accorded to articles imported by . . . Ministers . . . 'is not to be extended to the importations of . . . consuls' and this restriction has been contained in each subsequent edition of the general regulations under the customs and navigation laws." Treasury Decision, No. 9650, Oct. 5, 1889.

*1898:* Venezuela has refused free entry to official supplies sent to American consuls; reciprocal treatment ordered. Treasury Decision, No. 20086, Sept. 26, 1898. Likewise Japan. *Ibid.*, No. 20409, Oct. 13, 1898. Likewise when the Netherlands limited free entry to flags and escutcheons. *Ibid.*, Dec. 13, 1898.

*1915:* Art. 376. "The privilege of free entry is extended to the baggage and other effects of the following officials, their families, suites, and servants:

". . . consular officers accredited to this Government or en route to and from other countries to which accredited and whose Governments grant reciprocal privileges to American officials of like grade accredited thereto.

"Similar representatives of this Government abroad, including consular officers, returning from their missions.

"If by accident or unavoidable delay in shipment, the

baggage or other effects of a person of any of the classes mentioned in this article shall arrive after him, the same may be passed free of duty upon his declaration."

Art. 377. "Packages bearing the official seal of a foreign Government containing only official communications, documents, and office equipment, when accompanied by a certificate to that effect under such seal, may be admitted without customs examination. Costumes, regalia, and other articles for the official use of diplomatic and consular officers of a foreign Government will be admitted free of duty." *Customs Regulations,* 1915.

*1919:* In response to a request from the Danish minister the Secretary of State on Dec. 5, 1919 refused permission for the newly appointed consul at San Francisco to enter twenty boxes of wine, but accorded free entry privileges to sixty-two boxes of household goods and effects.

*1920:* In addition to the specifications of the Customs Regulations, *supra,* the Assistant Secretary of the Treasury ruled on Nov. 2, 1920 that "Packages of samples and other supplies bearing the official seal of a foreign Government are admitted free of duty and also, as above noted, similar packages without official seal, if for the official use of consular officers". A similar ruling was made on Oct. 16 of the same year.

*1923:* The new edition of the *Customs Regulations* contains in articles 404 and 405 the provisions of articles 376 and 377 of the edition of 1915.

The tendency in the past few years has been to emphasize the reciprocal nature of the privileges granted, and carefully to restrict them to consuls of those states which grant similar favors to American consuls within their borders.

In addition to the provisions designed to secure a general exemption from taxation, which might or might not include exemption from customs duties, five treaties with Mohammedan states have expressly stipulated for tariff exemption (Algiers, 1795, 1815, and 1816, Art. XVI; Tunis, 1797, Art. XVII; Egypt, 1884, Art. X). The usual provision is far different from this. While the convention relating to the Dutch colonies (1855, Art. XIII) expressly provides that the concessions granted shall never be construed to extend to customs duties, the customary phraseology has not mentioned specifically this type of taxation. Several of these general clauses have been interpreted to permit the levy of such taxes. This phase of taxation has already been considered in connection with the general tax exemption.[1]

### INCOME AND INHERITANCE TAXES

*Income Taxes.*[2]

It is only within comparatively recent years that states have come to place reliance upon income taxation as one of the chief sources of revenue. Because of that fact one finds little authority prior to the twentieth century on the question of consular exemption from this type of taxation. The examination of material incident to the present study of consular immunities has brought to light only a few instances. The Russian income tax law of 1851 extended to foreign consuls exemption from all Government or general and communal or local taxes and rates (*Reports relative to British Consular Establishments,* Vol. I: 176); the British consul at Turin, Italy, reported in 1871 an exemption from the Italian income tax (*ibid.*, I: 221); and a Dutch decree of June 25, 1885 exempted foreign consuls in the Netherlands from "local income taxes" (*Netherlands Consular Instructions* 1902, p. 38). As the practice of exempting consuls from certain types of taxes developed before income

[1] *Supra,* pp. 110-116.

[2] See p. 114, *supra,* for the provisions of the treaty of friendship, commerce, and consular rights, 1923, with Germany relative to income tax exemption.

taxation became prevalent, there is little occasion for surprise that attempts to secure exemption from these taxes have met with considerable opposition; and that where the exemption has been accorded, there is some confusion as to the basis upon which it should be placed.

The present century has witnessed the development of a practice in some states under which the exemption of consular officers from certain types of income taxation has been recognized. Especially has the United States been active in attempting to secure such exemptions. Most of the discussion which follows is based upon efforts of the United States in this regard.

In 1914 the American consul at Moncton, New Brunswick, protested against the levy of a $30.00 tax upon his official income. In reply to his protest Canadian officials informed him that British consuls in the United States, especially in New York and Boston, had been compelled to pay an income tax. The Secretary of State, instructing the consul on the point, stated on July 25 that "there appears to be no legal grounds which would justify you in refusing to pay the assessment complained of. . . . Moreover, the Department is not in a position to request of the British Government as a matter of comity your exemption from these local taxes, as it could give no guaranty of reciprocal treatment in a case of a levying of a like tax on a British consul, by one of the individual states of the United States."

The next phase in the development of the negotiations relative to Canadian income taxes appears to have come in 1920 when the employees of the consular office at Toronto were assessed for the income tax. This appears to have been a federal income tax, while that in the preceding case was provincial. Inasmuch as foreign consuls in the United States were not held liable to pay a federal tax on their official incomes, the United States requested that as a matter of comity the American consular officers be not subjected to Canadian income tax laws. It seems that as a matter of practice in Ontario, consuls and consuls general who objected to the payment of a tax upon their official incomes were exempted from such payment through the action of the assessor in marking " courtesy " in the payment column of the ledger. In the absence of the assessor, the consular officers were compelled to make returns.

Again in 1923 the American consul at Toronto was compelled to pay the Canadian income tax, because the Canadian authorities claimed they had no authority to release the consul from the payment. Negotiations between the two governments continued until the matter was brought to a conclusion by the passage of " an act to amend the income tax act of 1917 ", which became a law on June 30, 1923, and which provided that " the income of consuls and consuls general and of officials or officers of a foreign country whose duties require them to reside in Canada, if and only if they are citizens of the country they represent and are not engaged in any business or calling other than the duties appertaining to their official position, and provided that the country they represent grants a similar exemption to the officials of the government of Canada " were exempted from the payment of the income tax.

An attempt by the American government to get the British government to extend the " present exemption from the income tax of the official incomes of foreign consuls so as to include the private income of American consular officers derived from property located outside of the United Kingdom " showed that the official income was exempted. A memorandum prepared by the law officers of the Department in the course of the correspondence cited a statement made in 1887 to the effect that the Department was not aware that the income of any American consul derived from official sources, was taxed by the government of the country where he resided. *Foreign Relations,* 1909, pp. 284-286. The British Government refused the desired extension.

The Mexican Government, on the basis of reciprocity, has exempted consular officers from the decree of Feb. 24, 1924 fixing the income tax.

The Russian income-tax law of May 11, 1916 likewise provided for the exemption of consular officers from the operation of the tax on the basis of reciprocity.

While in 1911 Switzerland claimed the right to tax all consular officers, the American minister informed the Secretary of State on April 20, 1911 that the right had not been exercised in the case of American consular officers who were citizens of the United States. On June 3, 1921 the American chargé in Berne reported that no consular officer in Switzerland paid taxes, either federal or cantonal, on his official income. When the American consul general at Zurich on July 29, 1922 requested the Swiss authorities to issue a blanket exemption in favor of American vice consuls, the Government refused to do so; but did grant the desired exemption to all of the vice consuls by name.

The position of the American Department of State on April 12, 1911 as indicated in instructions to the consul at Karachi, India, was that " whatever we may say of the right of a Government to tax the incomes of persons residing within its borders as consuls from a foreign Government, the practice of late years of our own Government, and it is believed of the British Government, has not been to insist on such a tax. Therefore, whatever may be said of the abstract question of the right of the British Government to tax your income, you may with good reason claim exemption from such tax in the present case on the basis of international comity and reciprocal favor." This seems to have been the stand taken with reference to an attempt to tax the official income of the American consul at Calcutta in 1887. See Moore, *Digest,* V: 87.

The first income tax law passed by Congress made no provision for the exemption of the official income of consular officers. The Secretary of State, Seward, indicated to the Secretary of the Treasury on Sept. 23, 1863 that an amendment affording such an exemption would be highly desirable. Moore, *Digest,* V: 87. The suggestion was incorporated into an amendment of March 7, 1864 which extended the exemption not only to the official salary but also to such income as might be derived from property in other countries, on the basis of reciprocity. Statutes at Large, Vol. 13, pp. 14-17.

While the income tax laws passed under the Sixteenth Amendment have been interpreted to extend an exemption to the consular salary, consistent reasons have not been given by the Treasury Department as the basis for this exemption. Moreover, the extent of the exemption seems to have varied, though at present it seems to be confined to consuls of those states which grant a similar privilege to American consular officers. Thus, on Dec. 6, 1914, Secretary McAdoo wrote that " a tax upon their (consuls') official salaries or fees would be a tax upon the instrumentalities of the powers which they represent. It appears that it is a general rule of all governments to exempt from taxation the agencies of other governments necessary to carry into effect and secure diplomatic relations between the nations of the world. Replying, therefore, specifically to your inquiry, you are informed that the income of consular officers derived from their salaries or fees or from investments outside of the United States is exempt from the income tax."

This view was confirmed by a letter of April 20, 1918. On the other hand, the Treasury Department communicated to the Department of State on March 25, 1919 its view that "consuls and consuls general, as such, have no immunity from taxation by reason of their employment by foreign governments and, in regard to the tax liability are subject to the same rules as other individuals". After stating that salaries of diplomatic officers are exempted from the income tax under international comity, the letter concludes that consular officers do not have such a status. Under this view, the exemption of the consular salary depends entirely on whether the consul is a resident or a non-resident alien. So on June 29, 1920 the Assistant Secretary of the Treasury stated that "an alien who represents a foreign country in the capacity of a consular officer, although physically located in the United States, is not classified as a resident alien. His status for income tax purposes is that of a non-resident alien, and inasmuch as non-resident aliens are only subject to tax with respect to income derived from sources within the United States, such consular officers are subject to taxation only with respect to income derived from sources within the United States, exclusive of income received in their official capacity." The same attitude has been manifested in another letter of Feb. 6, 1920.

On May 21, 1923, however, the Department of the Treasury seems to have reverted to its original position as manifested in the McAdoo letter quoted above. "It is held by the Department that the place where personal services are rendered is the source of income regardless of the residence or character of the payer, of the place in which the contract for services was made, or of the place of payment. . . . Such exemption has been in accordance with the policy of the Department to exempt from taxation the salaries of agents of foreign governments who render services in this country in connection with legitimate governmental activities undertaken by such governments." While the letter specifically referred to Canadian immigration officers, the language is broad enough to include consuls.

On July 9, 1923 the Assistant Secretary of the Treasury ruled that Swedish consular officers and employees of Sweden at Swedish consulates in the United States who were Swedish citizens or subjects were exempted from taxation on the compensation received for their consular services, but did not restate the basis of the exemption.

Under a ruling of the Treasury Department made in 1925 all foreign consular officers and employees of foreign consulates in the United States who are nationals of the state appointing them, on the basis of reciprocity, are exempted from the payment of Federal income tax on the salaries, fees, and wages received by them in compensation for their consular services.

The situation with regard to treaty exemptions from income taxation has been set out above.[1]

If there is some doubt with regard to the exemption of the official income of consuls from taxation, the situation with regard to the private income of consuls offers still less to the consular officer. Hyde, *International Law,* Vol. I, paragraph 472, states that the Department of State in 1909 had declared that there was no legal obligation upon a foreign state to exempt an American consular officer from taxation upon his private income, even though derived from property situated in the United States. This view was substantiated on October 16, 1922 when the Secretary of State was of the opinion that "in the absence of applicable treaty provisions there is no rule of international law requiring the state to exempt a foreign consular officer from the payment of income tax on his private income. As a matter of comity, however, consular officers are usually exempted from the payment of tax on their private income derived from sources outside the state in which they perform their consular functions."

[1] *Supra,* pp. 110-116.

It may be noted in this connection that the attempt made in 1909 to get the British Government to extend the exemption from taxation of the official income to income derived from private sources outside of the British Empire did not meet with success. *Foreign Relations,* 1909, pp. 284-286.

The entire subject was reopened in 1922 in connection with a French law under which the American consul at Strassburg was taxed ten per cent of the interest on his current bank account. By the consular convention of 1853, American consuls in France were exempted from direct and personal taxes. The French Government maintained that the tax was collectible " due to the sole fact that a distribution of revenues has taken place under the items affected by the law, without considering the personality of the beneficiaries who enjoy these revenues. This tax has, therefore, according to French legislation, a *real* and *impersonal* character."

The Department of State was called upon to express its views on the direct nature of the taxation. After considering the cases of Pollock *vs.* Farmers' Loan and Trust Co., 157 U. S. 429; 158 U. S. 601; Brushaber *vs.* Union Pacific R. R., 240 U. S. 1; and Stanton *vs.* Baltic Mining Co., 240 U. S. 103, the Department was of opinion that income taxes are inherently indirect or excise taxes; that the Supreme Court in the Pollock case had taken income taxes from the class of excise taxes in which they inherently belonged and placed them in the category of direct taxes; and that the purpose of the Sixteenth Amendment was not to consider income taxes as direct taxes, but to prevent the court from resorting to the sources from which the taxes were derived. From this view of the decisions of the Supreme Court, the Department naturally concluded that income taxes could not properly be considered as direct taxes, and consequently did not in the United States fall within the category of direct taxes as specified by the consular convention.

Having failed to establish the nature of income taxes as direct taxes, the Department of State then offered to exempt from taxation income from personal bank accounts on a basis of reciprocity. To this the French minister of foreign affairs indicated he could not accede because of the repercussions that such an agreement might have upon the relations of France with other countries. The consul at Strassburg stated on July 20, 1922 that the tax was collected even upon coupons deposited in a Paris bank for transmission to a United States bank, there to be credited to the account of the consul.

It should be observed, as has been noted above,[1] that the United States has restricted the privilege of a consul to exemption from taxation on his official income to nationals of the appointing state. Although other tax exemptions are conditioned also upon the consul's being engaged in none other than the consular business, the most recent treaty, that of 1923 with Germany, extends the exemption from tax upon official salary even to those consuls engaged in a private occupation for gain when they are nationals of the states which has commissioned them.[2]

*Inheritance Taxes.*

There seems to be little available authority pertaining to the exemption of consular officers from inheritance taxes. Lehr, in his *Manuel,* sec. 1283, states that in France ready money and personal property of a consul, his wife, children, and foreign employees are exempted from inheritance taxes, but that the exemption does not extend beyond that point as all ministerial decisions on the matter expressly reserve the right of the treasury, notably on the succession of real property situated in France and upon French debts. This

[1] *Supra,* p. 132.

[2] *Supra,* pp. 113-115.

view is borne out by Bertheau, *Dictionaire Général de Droit et de Jurisprudence,* Vol. 4, No. 25416.

There are at least two instances of requests made in the United States for the exemption of property of deceased consuls from the operation of inheritance taxes. The first related to the estate of the deceased British consul at Portland, Oregon. In view of section 401 of the Revenue Act of 1918, providing for a tax on the "transfer of the net estate of every decedent dying after the passage of this Act, whether a resident or non-resident of the United States", the Solicitor of Internal Revenue had ruled that the property of decedents who were in the diplomatic or consular service of foreign countries was not exempted. Consequently, the Assistant Secretary of the Treasury reported on April 22, 1921 that the federal estate tax was to be levied upon the property. On April 25, 1921 the Inheritance Tax Department of Oregon pointed out that the Oregon tax was one imposed upon the privilege of taking by inheritance, ruling that there was nothing in the official character of the decedent which would entitle him to an exemption from a tax upon a privilege.

The second case involved the estate of a Norwegian consul general in New York, who had resigned in 1920 and who died in Norway in 1922. The Government of Norway indicated its willingness to enter into an agreement for the reciprocal waiving of the right to collect inheritance taxes in such cases. The reply of the Assistant Secretary of the Treasury to the Secretary of State on May 23, 1923 to a request for the position of the Department on this point indicated that the law did not make any provision for a waiver of the tax under any circumstances, and that consequently the United States Government was without power to enter into such a reciprocal agreement. Under the existing laws the Treasury Department had no option save to collect the tax. The President of the State Tax Commission of New York on May 29, 1923 in like manner informed the Secretary of State that there was no authority by which any person could waive collection of the New York inheritance tax.

In such cases it is obvious that the estate of the consular officer may be subject to three inheritance taxes: one United States federal, one United States state, and one in his native state. To these might be added still a fourth if the state commissioning the consul should have a federal form.

# CHAPTER V

## The Consul's Relation to Local Courts

Another group of exemptions arises from the consul's relation to the local courts. This relationship is threefold: a consul may be plaintiff, he may be defendant, and he may be called into court in connection with a suit between other persons. The consul as plaintiff has no need for special privilege; he may have access to the courts as other individuals. In connection with a suit in which he is not involved, the consul's usual contact with the local courts is in the capacity of witness. As defendant, the consul may be called upon to appear in civil and in criminal cases. A special phase of the latter has been treated below under the heading " Arrest and Imprisonment ".

### *The Consul as Witness*

A major point of contact between the consul and the judicial authorities of the state in which he is residing is afforded by the fact that parties to suits in the local courts are sometimes desirous of securing the evidence of the consular officer. Here again there must be a balance between the interests of the local government in the decision of disputes between its citizens and the interest of the appointing government in having its officer available for duty at specified periods. In the absence of a treaty stipulation this is a situation par excellence for the determination of the decision by the facts of the particular case.

At the outset it is to be noted that the rule of international law is that the consul is subject to be called as a witness, just as would be a private individual in possession of the same facts as those desired from the consul.[1] This, however, is subject to one definite qualification: the consul can not be called upon to testify as to the contents of the archives.[2] A further modification is sometimes introduced to the effect that the consul can not be compelled to testify as to information which came to him in his official capacity, as such information belongs to his government.[3] The ex-

[1] Mr. Hill, Secretary of State, to Mr. Hunter, minister to Guatemala, *Foreign Relations,* 1900, p. 705.

"You should appear as a witness and give your testimony unless you can get excused by the court on the ground that it will interfere with the performance of your official duties." Instructions to consul at Winnepeg, Dec. 1, 1910.

". . . a consular officer is not, in the absence of applicable treaty provisions, believed to be exempt from the giving of testimony with respect to matters not pertaining to his official consular business. The appropriate courts in this country would doubtless be disposed to give full consideration to the question whether foreign consular officers are exempt from the giving of testimony in cases in which the testimony of consular officers may be desired." Department of State, to minister of Poland, March 22, 1924. The Polish minister had indicated his opinion that there was a "custom accepted by international law of exempting consuls from the obligation to appear as witnesses before the courts in the states in which they discharge their duties."

The same idea was expressed by Secretary Marcy in 1855; see Moore, *Digest,* vol. v, p. 20. See also United States *v.* Trumbull, 48 Fed. 94 (1891) and *Foreign Relations,* 1905, pp. 458-460.

[2] For this qualification and its implication, see page 38, *supra.*

[3] "As regards your statement that you are instructed to claim inviolability for the archives, it is observed that the Bombay authorities in their letter to you of April 4th expressly recognize the inviolability of the archives and property of the consulate. Should you again be requested to appear in court as a witness and to produce official archives you will not only claim exemption from producing said consular documents, but also from giving testimony in respect to official consular business." Department of State to consul at Bombay, Oct. 21, 1919.

"Under the general rules of international law a consul may not be summoned to give evidence concerning consular business or to produce

tension seems to be justified. Protection of the archives is afforded not only to prevent the interruption of consular business due to a possible absence of consular records, but also because the archives are information of the government which the consul has no authority to reveal. This last applies as well to the case of knowledge acquired in an official capacity. Here, too, the consul must be the judge in the first instance of the fact whether the information came to him in an official capacity; the receiving government has its interests protected in the right to apply to the consul's government for the information and in that of revoking the consul's exequatur if it feels that he is abusing his official position.

Where the consul is called as a witness, the practice is for the summons to be in the nature of a request rather than in

to the court any part of the consular archives; and information which came to him in his official capacity, he is privileged from disclosing, for such information belongs to his government.

"He can not be required to divulge information which came to him in his official capacity, for that is the exclusive property of his government; but as to matters which come within his knowledge or observation in his mere capacity as an individual he is not privileged from testifying as a witness. If a consul should himself participate in the commission of a crime or in setting on foot an insurrection, or should observe others doing so, against the Government to which he is accredited, he could not be shielded from testifying, according to the forms of the local law, as to the facts thus acquired and within his knowledge." Hay, Sec. of State, to Mr. Merry, minister to Nicaragua, April 17, 1899. *Foreign Relations,* 1899, p. 567.

In 1922 the American consul at Santiago, Cuba, was requested to testify in the trial of a Cuban official alleged to have misappropriated funds. As the only information the consul had came to him in his official capacity, he declined to appear without the authorization of his Government. His position was sustained by the Department of State: ". . . It is a generally recognized principle that such officers (consuls) cannot be summoned to give evidence coming to them in their official capacity. In view of this practice, the Department considers that you were justified in your declination to appear in court to testify in the case in question."

the usual form of a command carrying a penalty for failure to comply; [1] and at least one state goes so far as to provide

[1] In 1899 the American consul general at Frankfort on the Main, Germany, was served with a subpoena to appear as a witness in a case then pending before the royal court. The subpoena contained the clause: "Witnesses who do not appear without sufficient excuse are to be sentenced, according to paragraph 50 of the penal code, to pay the costs occasioned by such non-appearance, also to a fine not to exceed 300 marks; and if this is not paid, to imprisonment not to exceed six weeks—producing them by arrest is also admissible." The consul general protested vigorously against the threat of arrest but notified the court that he was willing to appear if properly summoned. The matter was taken up by the Department of State, and in the course of the negotiations it was shown that in spite of the fact that the consular offices were inviolable, the consul was threatened with arrest and imprisonment outside of his office in case he failed to obey the summons—the only other alternative being that the consul remain constantly in his office. A satisfactory conclusion of the affair was reached when the German officials apologized for their mistake in sending out the subpoena in the usual form, and politely requested the presence of the consul general in court. Moore, *Digest*, vol. v, p. 81.

In 1905 the American consul at Solingen, Germany, was served with a subpoena in usual form. He refused to appear, but agreed to do so if his presence were requested. The request was made and the incident closed. *Foreign Relations*, 1905, pp. 458-460.

In 1914 the American consul at Catania, Italy, protested the terms of a subpoena in regular form, indicating at the same time his willingness to appear if requested. The local authorities immediately apologized, stating that the official character was not known to the person preparing the subpoena.

When in August of 1916 the American consul at Newcastle, Australia, was constrained to obey a preemptory subpoena to give evidence in a petty case, the clearance of an American vessel was delayed one day as a result. In reply to the protest of the government of the United States that "international practice concedes to consular officials such privileges and immunities as are necessary to enable them properly to discharge the duties of their office and that peremptory summons such as complained of by the consul at Newcastle do not seem to accord with such international practice," the British government sent its regrets, stating that no discourtesy was intended, but said nothing of discontinuing the practice. On March 19, 1918 the consul was again served with a summons in the usual form; being extremely busy with a departing ship, he did not immediately attend court. Nothing was done.

that if compliance with the citation would interfere unduly with the consular business, the consul may notify that fact to the judge, and the latter will provide for the taking of the consul's deposition.[1]

Care is taken in the laws of some states to see that the consul has ample notice of the time and place at which he is to appear. This would seem advisable, though in many states the ordinary rules governing the appearance of witnesses are sufficient to enable the consul to make provision for the necessary absence from his office.[2]

There is some precedent for the view that consuls can not be compelled to appear as witnesses before a court-martial; though there seems to be no justification in theory for such an exception, it has been recognized in at least one Central American country.[3]

[1] Mexican law of 1859, article 18, section XI. Likewise, the Haitian law of 1912 provides if the consul is unable to present himself before the court, an officer of the court is to repair to the consular dwelling to obtain the testimony viva voce. Art. 26.

That this indulgence granted by Mexico is not to be claimed as a matter of right under international law is indicated in Article 55C of the Regulations of 1923 which state that exemption from personal appearance in local courts to testify in civil or criminal cases is accorded in certain countries, but on a basis of local legislation or custom.

[2] Honduras, law on foreign consuls, art. 47; Salvador, *ibid.*, art. 49; Mexico, law of 1859, art. 18, sec. XI.

[3] ". . . I arrived at the conclusion that such evidence could not be properly given before a court-martial. The English vice-consul taking the same ground, appeared, and after giving his name and address, refused to testify without the order of his superior, who has supported him. I was also influenced by the desire to avoid a dangerous precedent. Martial law is often declared in the Spanish-American Republics during time of peace, as at Bluefields, for political purposes. If these military courts are authorized to demand the presence of our consular officers as witnesses there is no limit to the possibility of abuse resulting therefrom, as no restriction will be placed by them upon the information they will ask for, and the privileged consular information will thus be accessible to them. In the case of Mr. Clancey it was doubly dangerous,

Of course, there is no reason why a consul on leave in the territory of the state which has appointed him should be exempted from appearing as a witness in its courts; and the proper authorities in the United States have so held.

Treaty provisions governing the action of consuls as witnesses were late in appearing. Though the first consular convention entered into by the United States came in 1788, no mention of the consul as witness is to be found before 1850; and then the statement was simply that whenever the presence of a consular officer was required in court, he should be requested in writing to appear. The consular convention of 1853 with France provided that when the testimony of consuls was desired, they should be requested in writing to appear; and if they were unable to do so, their testimony should be taken in writing or orally at the consular dwelling. Compulsory process might not issue. Dillon's case [1] re-

because, not understanding Spanish, he would have no means of knowing if his evidence was correctly translated. Instances have occurred recently at Bluefields where the hired Government translator tried to have recorded what the foreign witness had not stated, but, the witness understanding Spanish, he was promptly corrected and reprimanded by the witness. The matter having been practically closed, and no demand made upon me for consular evidence after my arrival at Bluefields, the precedent is now established that before courts-martial in Central America ministers and consular officers need not testify—a position which I respectfully suggest may be of importance hereafter." Mr. Merry, United States minister to Nicaragua, to Mr. Hay, Sec. of State, May 9, 1899. *Foreign Relations*, 1899, p. 583. Mr. Merry's action was taken before the receipt of instructions from the Secretary of State; those instructions had made no distinction between civil courts and courts-martial with regard to the consul's liability to testify, but had made the usual distinction between official and non-official information. Therefore, it can not be said that the American Government has gone on record in favor of such a distinction as that made by its minister; the incident had already been closed, and the matter was simply allowed to drop. All of the reasons advanced by Mr. Merry for his opposition to consular testimony in courts-martial apply with equal force to testimony before civil courts in the same country.

[1] See *infra*, p. 144.

sulted; and it was contended that the Sixth Amendment to the United States Constitution secured to defendants in criminal cases compulsory process for witnesses in their behalf. Though the contention was adversely disposed of by the trial judge, all later conventions which have treated this point have made reservations in favor of the cases contemplated by this amendment.

As the summary of treaty provisions shows, an attempt has been made to protect the consular functions from interference when the consul is called as a witness in a civil case. If he can comply with the request for his appearance without interfering with his official duties, it is incumbent upon him to do so. However, if personal appearance should be detrimental to the consular business, the consul may decline to appear; and in that case, his testimony is to be taken orally or in writing at his office or residence.

The differences in the treaty provisions are with reference to the consul's obligation in criminal cases. Avoidance of any basis for a contention of conflict with the Sixth Amendment has guided the framing of these provisions; Dillon's cases of the future are to be avoided. This is accomplished primarily through the requirement that in criminal cases contemplated by the Sixth Amendment, compulsory process may issue. While this is as far as it is necessary to go in order to avoid the possible conflict, it is not as far as some treaties have gone, nor is it as far as it is desirable to go. State constitutions usually make provision for compulsory process in favor of defendants in criminal cases; a treaty which provided simply for compulsory process in cases contemplated by the Sixth Amendment to the federal Constitution would conflict with every such state constitutional provision. While the treaty as the supreme law of the land would prevail, it seems simpler to avoid the conflict; and some treaties have extended the compulsory process to cases contemplated by such state constitutional provisions.

A few treaties have couched the provision in entirely different language, permitting compulsory process to issue in all criminal cases at the request of the defendant. This eliminates the necessity for an interpretation of constitutional provisions to ascertain just how far the compulsory process extends. The recent treaty with Germany goes a step farther and extends the compulsory process to its logical limits, in that it permits compulsory process to issue at the request of the prosecution as well as of the defense. There seems to be no compelling reason why the defense should be placed in a better position than the prosecution in the calling of witnesses. It is to be hoped that all later provisions on this subject will be drawn along the lines of the German treaty.

Not many treaties have carried provisions on this point as the following summary shows:

1. Whenever the presence of consuls is required in courts of justice, they shall be summoned in writing.

Colombia, CC, 1850: V.[1]

2. Never be compelled to appear as witnesses. When declaration for judicial purposes, or deposition, is to be received from them in the administration of justice, they shall be invited in writing to appear; if unable to do so, their testimony shall be requested in writing or taken orally at dwelling.

France, CC, 1853: II.[2]

[1] Colombian consuls are entitled to participate in the French provision (next following) under the most-favored-nation clause. United States *v.* Trumbull, 1891, 48 Fed. 94.

[2] In the April session, 1854, of the United States district court for the northern district of California, the French consul at San Francisco was served with a subpoena *duces tecum* in a criminal case in which the defense wished to secure him as a witness. When the consul failed to appear in court, he was brought in under attachment; but the court released him after further consideration of the Sixth Amendment to the United States Constitution, coming to the conclusion that the object of that amendment was fulfilled if the defendant enjoyed equal rights with

3. Not compelled to appear as witnesses. When testimony is needed, consul shall be invited in writing to appear; if unable, testimony shall be taken in writing or orally at dwelling or office. Consul's duty to comply without any delay which can be avoided. In all criminal cases under Sixth Amendment to United States Constitution, appearance shall be demanded, with all possible regard to consular dignity and to duties of office. A similar treatment shall be accorded to United States consuls in the contracting state in like cases.

Italy, CC, 1868: IV; CC, 1878: IV.
Belgium, CC, 1868: IV; CC, 1880: IV.
Servia, CC, 1881: IV.
Roumania, CC, 1881: IV.
Sweden, CC, 1910: IV.

4. Same as 3 except that compulsory process is extended to cases contemplated by the Sixth Amendment to the United States Constitution and similar provisions in state constitutions and that the compulsory clause is not made reciprocal.

Netherlands, CC, 1878: IV.
Greece, CC, 1902: IV.
Spain, F&GR, 1902: XVI.

5. Not summoned as witnesses except when, pursuant to law,

the government in compelling the attendance of witnesses (In re Dillon, Fed. Cas. 3,914). The French Government entered a vigorous protest against the treatment accorded its consul. Secretary of State Marcy contended that the constitutional provision nullified the treaty immunity so far as the two conflicted; but when the French Government persisted in its stand, the American Government officially expressed its regret at the court's action, and saluted a French national ship in accordance with the terms of a compromise reached by the two governments (Moore, *Digest*, vol. v, pp. 78-80). Dana says that the point was finally settled by instructions from the French Government to its consuls to obey the subpoena in similar cases which might arise in the future (Dana's Wheaton, p. 325). This incident led to a note by Secretary of State Fish in 1872 in which he commented on the necessity for avoiding any such inconsistency in the future treaties. He referred with approval to the provision in the Italian consular convention of 1868 (next following). Wharton, *Digest*, vol. i, p. 777.

testimony may be necessary to defense of person charged with crime. In other cases, when testimony is deemed necessary, court shall go to consular dwelling to have testimony taken orally, or shall send officer to reduce it to writing, or shall ask of him a written declaration.

Austria-Hungary, CC, 1870: III.

6. Not compelled to appear as witness. When testimony is needed, it shall be asked in writing, or officer shall go to his house or take it viva voce. If testimony is necessary for defense of person charged with crime and should not be voluntarily given, compulsory process requiring the presence of the consul may be issued.

Salvador, AC&CP, 1870: XXXV.

7. In criminal cases attendance of consular officer as witness may be demanded by prosecution or defense, with all possible regard for consular dignity and duties; consular officer shall comply. In civil cases testimony taken orally or in writing at residence or office, and with due regard to convenience of consul; officer should voluntarily give his testimony at trial whenever possible to do so without serious interference with his official duties.

Germany, FC&CR, 1923: XVIII.

Even where these exemptions are given, however:

it is the duty of the consul, when invited to appear in court to give his testimony, to comply with the request unless *he is unable to do so*. This duty he violates, if he refuses without good and substantial excuse. Not his official character, his disinclination, nor any slight personal inconvenience constitutes such an excuse. The pressure and importance of official duties requiring immediate performance may prevent his attendance in court, but such can rarely be the case where the court sits at the place of his residence. It is not claimed that the court can entertain the question of the competency of his excuse for declining to comply with its invitation; but, where the government of the United States has fair grounds to question the good faith with which the consul avails himself of the provisions of the convention which exempts him from compulsory process, it has two modes of redress and it can take either at its option. It may appeal to the consul's government to inquire into the case in this respect, and to deal with him as it shall find his conduct deserves, or it may revoke his exequatur.[1]

## *Liability to Suit*

Today there can be no doubt about a consul's liability to suit. A single exception to that rule has been noted.[2]

[1] Marcy, Sec. of State, to Mr. Figaniere, March 27, 1855; Moore, V: 81. The same idea is brought out in the *Consular Regulations* (1896), p. 32.

[2] The British pro-consul at Panama in 1833 became involved in difficulties with a citizen of New Granada. As a result of the anti-British feeling at the time, the consul was sentenced to six years in prison for carrying a concealed weapon, when the charge of assault brought against him failed; and the court refused to consider a counter-case brought by the consul. The consulate was entered and an armed guard placed there to secure the consul who was too ill to be removed to prison. (He was removed as soon as he had sufficiently recovered.) In reply to a British demand for the release of the consul and the removal of officials concerned with his imprisonment, the government refused to interfere with the judicial action, claiming that it had no constitutional right to do so. The English proceeded to blockade and the Government of New Granada prepared for war. It was under these circumstances that the supreme court to which the case had gone handed down its opinion, in which it was held that the lower court had not properly considered the question of its jurisdiction. When the case was sent back to the lower court, the consul was released after an imprisonment of eleven months and fifteen days, with an indemnity of 1000 pounds. The following extracts from the opinion of the lower court in freeing the officer indicate the reason therefor: "That the most standard authors such as Martens allow immunity to consuls and vice consuls, this being moreover, the established practice among Nations for the last twenty years." "That the same supreme court of justice of the Republic in the aforesaid resolution (of October 25, 1883) declared that the French consul, Adolphe Barrot, prosecuted for want of respect to the first alcalde of the cathedral ward of the City of Carthagana, enjoyed immunities." "That in the same act referred to, the court declared itself incompetent to proceed against consuls not only in civil but also in criminal cases." "That the pre-

However, a distinction must be made between the cases involving action of the consul in his official capacity and those which concern the consul personally. In the first type of cases, some courts hold that the consul may not be sued. Thus the French courts refused to entertain a suit against an English consul for slander when the consul defended himself on the grounds that the remarks complained of were made by him in his official capacity and in the conduct of the consular business. "It would be impossible for consuls to have the necessary freedom of action for the discharge of their duties if they could be subject to prosecution by their own countrymen before French courts for acts they had done or even for remarks they had made in their official capacity." [1]

Warden [2] cites a case given in Merlin's *Répertoire Universal* where the problem is stated as follows: "Can foreign consuls be prosecuted before our tribunals for acts done in France by order of their government and with the authorization of the French government? The imperial attorney-general has declared after a thorough examination of the subject that the negative is incontestable and that this opinion has been consecrated by a decision of the Court of Cassation

cedent of the supreme court declaring itself incompetent in a similar case (that of the above mentioned French consul) when perhaps it was the only one entitled to act in the present question, leaves no tribunal in the Republic to which resort can be had." *British and Foreign State Papers*, vol. xxvi, pp. 128-268.

It is very probable that this extraordinary decision was the result of the diplomatic situation at the time.

[1] Case of Lee Jortin, *JDIP*, 1900, pp. 130-132, 958-964; Stowell and Munro, *International Cases*, vol. i, pp. 26-30. *Pandects Françaises*, vol. xxi, pp. 379-380 contain references to a number of cases in which a similar conclusion has been reached. That there is no immunity for personal acts, see nos. 91, 92, 128-130 and 140-144. For illustrations of immunity from suit involving official acts, see nos. 123-125.

[2] *Consular Establishment*, pp. 109-112.

of the third vendemiaire, ninth year." The decision of the court was in accord with the contention of the attorney-general.

The reason given by the French courts in making the distinction is this: The consul in performing his official acts is proceeding under the authority of his government and the court in permitting a suit against the consul would in fact be allowing a suit against the government which appointed the consul. Furthermore, inasmuch as the consul in receiving his exequatur is authorized by the government which receives him to perform his functions, the official act is one done with the authorization of the receiving as well as the appointing government.[1] No record has been found to indi-

[1] The organic law of the diplomatic and consular service of Salvador directs Salvadorean consular officers to "claim as essential for the service of their charge . . . the freedom of those acts appropriate to their consular character." Article 93. To the same effect is Bolivia, Regulations, 1887, art. 21, Regulations, 1877, art. 11; Chile, Regulations, 1915, art. 113, Regulations, 1860, art. 17; Costa Rica, Regulations, 1888, article 27; Honduras, Law on Foreign Consuls, art. 40; Liberia, Regulations, art. 113; Salvador, Law on Foreign Consuls, art. 42; Uruguay, Regulations, 1917, art. 57, Regulations, 1906, art. 72, Regulations, 1878, art. 56. And see, *Diccionario de la Jurisprudencia Argentina*, I: 445. In addition the following states have similar provisions:

*Dominican Republic:* "Independence belonging to their consular character" is to be claimed by consuls of the Republic as essential to the exercise of their functions. *Ley*, 1887, art. 18.

*Ecuador:* Regulations 1870, art. 17 identical with Dominican Republic.

*France:* French courts have held that consuls can not be hailed before them for debts contracted by them in their official capacity. "It is an absolute immunity, always recognized; it rests on the consideration that the consul represents, in the exercise of his functions, the sovereign authority of the country which has named him: now to control the acts of the consul done in this character, would be to submit to the jurisdiction of the local tribunals, the foreign State which the consul represents." *Pandects Françaises*, vol. 21, p. 380, no. 123; and decisions cited in nos. 124, 125.

*Mexico:* Immunity from jurisdiction for official acts is granted under international law. Regulations, 1923, art. 53E.

*Russia:* "They (consuls) may not be judged by the Soviet Russian

cate that the Government of the United States has recognized this distinction.[1]

Among the different cases involving this point which have arisen may be noted one arising in 1913 in which the American vice consul at Milan, Italy, had discharged his clerk without notice in advance. The latter brought suit for his salary because of the lack of notice. The defendant refused to appear in court, claiming that the tribunal had no authority over his official acts. The American ambassador informed the Secretary of State on June 6 that when the matter was taken up diplomatically, the Ministry of Foreign Affairs and the Ministry of Justice both indicated that the tribunal was one which neither could approach. The case was finally dismissed by the court because of improper designation of the defendant as a representative of the Department of State of America, the petition not indicating what republic of America. The court declined to pass on the question of its jurisdiction, and the consul steadily refused to appear.

When in 1910 two British seamen brought suit in a Cuban court against a British consul on a set of facts arising out of an official act of the consul, the British Government

Courts for wrong-doing or exceeding the rights of their full powers. This must be brought before the National Commissariat for Foreign Affairs to be tried and settled by diplomatic means." Summary of a decree of the Soviet Government published in Moscow *Isvestia,* for July 7, 1921.

[1] When a foreign consul in the United States performs a duty in accordance with his official capacity, the courts of this country are not inclined to investigate the case. So, when a person comes into court seeking to secure a review of a consul's official acts, the court will not assume jurisdiction if the parties are soon to be within the jurisdiction of their national courts (The Infanta, 1848, Fed. Cas. 7,030; Saunders *v.* The Victoria, 1854, Fed. Cas. 12,377). But when the parties will not be so situated that there can be a prompt settlement by the national tribunals, the courts of the United States will review the act in question (Patch *v.* Marshall, 1853, Fed. Cas. 10,793; Lorway *v.* Lousada, 1856, Fed. Cas. 8,517).

took the matter up with the political branch of the Cuban Government. The latter transmitted the British note to the supreme court. Though the court expressly refrained from passing on the particular question, its decision carried the following:

> Notwithstanding all this, there is no objection to admitting, with a view to avoiding future difficulties, the claim that charges made against foreign consuls should not be recognized by the judges when it is evident that the matter in complaint is an act performed by the consul in his official character for which he is responsible to his Government alone, since in conformity with the principles of international law consular officers are not subject to the jurisdiction of the courts of the countries to which they are accredited in respect of acts performed in the exercise of their official character and in the name of the Government that they represent, as the British minister states in his note as the basis of the claim.
>
> It is agreed therefore to advise the judges . . . that they should not recognize charges that are made before them against foreign consular officers when it is evident that the matter which is the object of the complaint does not come within the jurisdiction of the Cuban courts because the act performed by the consul was done in his official character for which he is responsible to his Government alone." (The decision is published in No. 128 of the *Gaceta Oficial*, p. 5623.)

The more usual type of case seems to be one in which a creditor of an employee of the consul attempts to secure an attachment of the salary due the employee. Such a case arose in 1912 involving the American consul general in Berlin. When the consul general protested against the attachment proceeding, the court stated that the creditor had claimed that his debtor had been in the personal service of the consul, and immediately dismissed the attachment proceeding. Consul General, Berlin, to Secretary of State, Oct. 3, 1912.

A similar case occurred in Maracaibo, Venezuela in May of 1913. The matter was prevented from being carried to its final conclusion by the resignation of the clerk. On June 7, 1913 the Secretary of State wrote: "In reply to your request for further instructions . . . you are informed that there is no doubt that consular officers are subject generally to the jurisdiction of the local courts, but the question here raised appears to be whether the funds of this Government in the hands of a consular officer, due to a clerk in the consulate, can be garnished by proceedings in the local courts. You are instructed that this Government does not recognize the right of the Venezuelan courts to exercise control of the moneys of this Government in your possession due as salary of the clerk of the consul."

One result of the consul's residence is that the territorial court is the one to pass upon the character of the act which is being challenged. Where consuls are not liable to suits for their official acts, there remains the problem of determining what acts are official. In the first instance, the determination of the question rests with the court in which the suit is filed.[1] This determination, however, is subject to a review in diplomatic negotiations which will arise if the court's decision is believed to be incorrect.

It is believed that no state today maintains an exemption of consular officers from suits brought against them in their private capacity. The usual formula in the Regulations is "In civil and criminal matters, consuls are subject to the laws of the place of their residence". Where no comment is made in the following list, that formula, or a slight modification of it is used:

*Argentina:* Regulations, 1906, art. 62; 1862, arts. 10 and

[1] For a difference in the interpretation of the official character of particular acts, compare *Pandects Françaises*, vol. xxi, p. 380, no. 125, and Jamar, 1814-1880, vol. iii, p. 96, no. 8.

29. For a digest of judicial decisions on the point, see *Diccionario de la Jurisprudencia Argentina,* I: 445.

*Belgium:* Regulations for the Congo, art. 4.

*Bolivia:* Regulations, 1887, arts. 27 and 103; the latter refers to foreign consuls in Bolivia.

*Brazil:* See *British and Foreign State Papers,* 42: 1316 for the imperial decree of 1851.

*Chile:* Regulations, 1915: art. 112; 1897, art. 36.

*Colombia: Guía,* p. 104, containing Law of 1866, art. 39. A law of May 10, 1834 gave to the supreme court jurisdiction in cases, civil or criminal, involving consuls "to whom by treaty has been conceded the character of diplomatic agents". But no treaties have given such a character; therefore, jurisdiction goes to certain inferior courts having a residual jurisdiction.

*Costa Rica:* Regulations, 1888, art. 31.

*Cuba: Instrucciones Provisionales,* pp. 6 and 7.

*Denmark:* Circular of 1821, contained in Bursotti, I: 163. *Consular Instructions,* par. 86: Consuls have "no justifiable claim to be exempt from the laws and jurisdiction of the country."

*France:* There is no immunity from suit for personal acts, and the personal property of the consul may be seized, as a matter of precaution, in a suit brought against him for debt. *Pandects Françaises,* Vol. 21, p. 379, nos. 90, 96, 129-139.

*Germany:* Law of Judicial Organization, quoted in Ozanam, *L'Immunité Civile de Juridicion des Agents Diplomatiques,* p. 72; also Bursotti, II: 515.

*Greece:* Instructions, 1834, Art. 3, par. 7, contained in Bursotti, II: 515.

*Guatemala: Apéndice al Reglamento Consular,* par. 5a, contained in Saravia, *Derecho Patrio.*

*Honduras:* Regulations, 1906, art. 33.

*Paraguay,* Regulations, 1871, arts. 12, 38.

*Peru: Guía Peruanos,* Vol. I, p. 511; Regulations, 1897, art. 28; 1863, art. 12.

*Russia:* On December 1, 1871 the British consul at Taganrog reported that "with reference to jurisdiction all are amenable to the Russian Courts of Justice". *Reports relative to British Consular Establishments,* II: 126.

A summary of the decree of the Soviet Government stating the position of foreign consuls was published in *Isvestia* according to a despatch in the London *Times* of July 19, 1921. According to the summary sent by the consul at Viborg, Finland, on July 28, 1921 liability to suit remains.

*Salvador: Cartilla Consular,* sec. 23.

*Uruguay:* Regulations, 1917, sec. 56; 1906, sec. 71; 1878, art. 40.

*United States:* Regulations, 1896, sec. 73; 1888, sec. 50; 1881, sec. 77; 1868, secs. 13 and 18; General Instructions, 1855, sec. 6. See page 26 *supra* for the opinion of Attorney General Wirt that consuls are liable to civil suits.

In federal states provision is sometimes made for the exclusive jurisdiction of the federal courts in cases involving foreign consuls.[1] The Argentine provision in this connection is unique in that cases involving the immunities of consuls are reserved for the supreme court, while the lower courts have jurisdiction over other cases involving consuls.[2]

There are no treaties of the United States which relieve

[1] Constitution of the United States, art. iii. The exclusive jurisdiction of federal courts established in 1789 (1st Cong., 1st Sess., ch. xx, sec. ix) was lost in the revision of 1875, and from that date until 1911 state and federal courts exercised concurrent jurisdiction. The judicial code of 1911 (61st Cong., 3rd Sess., ch. 231, secs. 24, 256) restored the exclusive jurisdiction. See In re Iasigi, 79 Fed. 751, on the general question of jurisdiction; and Gittings *v.* Crawford, Fed. Cas. 5,465.

[2] *Diccionario de la Jurisprudencia Argentina,* I: 445.

a consul from liability to suit. The fact that there are no such provisions is strong evidence of a belief that this type of immunity is hardly to be desired. A clause establishing a residual liability of consuls [1] throws a little light on the point and that little favors the retention of the liability.

*Arrest and Imprisonment*

That a complete subjection of the consul to the operation of the laws of the state in which he is resident would involve submission to arrest when decreed by those laws can not be open to doubt. Nor can it be questioned that such arrest must operate as an important restriction upon the freedom of action necessary to the fulfillment of the consular functions, and consequently is not to be undertaken without good reason. It would seem that the desire of a state to maintain to the fullest extent the operation of its civil and criminal laws and its expectation that its consuls abroad will be given such freedom as is necessary for their duties, together with the realization that reciprocity must play a large part in the adjustment of these two possibly conflicting principles, would result in a compromise which would at least exempt the consul from arrest when such exemption would not involve any serious delay or danger of the defeat of the operation of the laws. However, the practice of nations can not be said to have evolved any definite rule on this point.

In endeavoring to ascertain what should be the governing principle it must be borne in mind that the exemption, if any is to exist, is that of the government in order that the consular functions may be performed and is not personal to the consul and so to be imposed by the consul to shield himself from the effects of his actions unconnected with his official position.

Civil arrest is defined as " the apprehension of a person by

[1] See page 190, *infra*.

virtue of a lawful authority to answer the demand against him in a civil action ". As the purpose of the arrest is to assure the presence of the defendant, there seems to be little reason why the process should be applied to a consular officer. His position is in itself a guarantee of his presence. He is stationed at his post by his government; and that government will require his services at the post until he is relieved. In this situation, further assurance of his presence would seem to be unnecessary.

Arrest and imprisonment in civil cases have usually been the outcome of an action to recover a debt; this clearly is not a matter of such compelling urgency that the creditor's state should interrupt the discharge of the consular functions in order to secure the immediate punishment of the debtor. The creditor will not receive an earlier payment as a result of such action; other citizens have sufficient protection in their right to refuse to extend credit to the offending consul. The matter can be called to the attention of the appointing government, which can either bring pressure to bear upon the delinquent to compel the payment of the debt or make arrangements to supersede him. In the latter case there can be no objection to the operation of the local laws as soon as the consul's government has arranged for the continuance of the consular office. Such a procedure is sufficient to protect the interests of both states and of the individuals concerned, and still does not subject the appointing government to the embarrassment of interrupted consular activities. The question does not seem to have given rise to any important negotiations.[1] Inasmuch as there is a dearth of authority on this point, it is probable that the character of the men appointed to the consular office is such that the

[1] However, in 1861 Secretary Seward stated that the law of nations as applied in the United States did not exempt a consul from arrest for debt. Wharton, *Digest*, I: 776.

cases rarely arise, or that the disposition of such cases under the local laws has not occasioned any interference with the consular functions—in other words that civil arrest has not been resorted to when such action would inconvenience the consul's government.

The problem of criminal arrest is more serious. While it is true that the effect of arrest and imprisonment on the consular office would not be more deplorable in the case of criminal than of civil arrest, it is also true that the effectiveness of the criminal laws is dependent in large part upon the restraint of the offender following their violation. Even in this case, however, it would seem advisable that so far as practicable the appointing government should be permitted to protect its consular interests. No objection can be imposed to the consul's being committed to prison for criminal offenses; such is the necessary result of his subjection to the local laws. Nor should a privilege which is that of his government protect him from his punishment. This, however, does not dispose of the question, for there still remains the problem of adjusting the operation of the penalty to the interests of the government whose interests the official represents. And this is as true of the preliminary arrest as of the final punishment.

In the nature of things the question must be resolved in the first instance by the government whose laws have been broken; and much should depend upon the nature of the offense. Immediate arrest should be resorted to only when necessary to prevent further violation of the laws, when necessary to protect the consul, or when there is ground for believing that the officer will use his freedom to flee from the jurisdiction. In these cases the interests of the offended government are believed to be paramount; it can not be expected to sit by in peace and suffer the open violation of its laws. Other cases do not call for such immediate action, and the interests of the appointing government may be protected without danger of further infraction of the laws of the receiving state. Such protection is accorded if the consul is admitted to bail and so is permitted his liberty for the performance of his functions until his government has had time to replace him. Of course, if the appointing government should see fit not to make other provision for the consular office, such action is equivalent to a waiver of the extension in its favor, and the suit may be prosecuted exactly as any other criminal action.

Where the arrest is unwarranted as is sometimes the case when there is a revolution in progress or in times of violent excitement, the incident is usually made the subject of diplomatic protest, and if the circumstances warrant, of a claim for reparations. This has no connection with the consul's subjection to criminal jurisdiction; it is simply the exercise of the right of a state to expect that its officers will be protected in the performance of their duties.[1]

In the absence of treaty provision no record has been found where a state has recognized the exemption of consuls from criminal arrest. The following extracts from official

[1] Martens, in his *Causes Célèbres*, cites an instance of such an indignity to a French consul in Venezuela in 1833; proper apologies were made and salutes given. Volume VI: 554-567.

An aggravated instance involving the British pro-consul at Panama in 1833 is given in *British and Foreign State Papers*, 26: 128-268. One thousand pounds indemnity was paid in this instance.

A number of similar incidents arose out of the Mexican revolutions of 1910-1920. In these cases the treatment of the consuls was the result of an anti-Amercan feeling which was visited against the consuls together with other Americans because of their nationality. See, for example, *Foreign Relations*, 1914, p. 657.

Jenkin's Case (Hyde, *Int. Law*, I: 504-505) is an example of an unusual perversion of justice in that the consul was arrested when he was the injured party, the charge obviously being a blind. The United States intervened to protect its consul without waiting for that officer to exhaust the local remedies.

documents show the general attitude on the subject (where no comment is made, the provision is simply that the consul is subject to criminal jurisdiction with no provision for special treatment):

*Belgium:* While consuls are subject to the civil and commercial tribunals and to penal proscriptions like all other foreigners, the regulations for the Congo provide "It is expedient to treat them with the regard due their official character. They can not be arrested, except in case of absolute necessity, and the magistrates will use, concerning them, all the consideration compatible with the proper administration of justice." *Foreign Relations,* 1887: 26-29.

*Brazil:* Under the imperial decree of 1851 foreign consuls might be imprisoned without authority from the imperial government only in cases of unbailable offenses; and the trial would be held in Brazil only when "by reason of the circumstances with which the crime is attended, or for a weighty reason, they should not deliver such agent to the Government of which he is a subject, to be tried in his own country, or that it should not be sufficient to send him out of the country, or to deprive him of his exequatur." Articles XVII, XVIII in *British and Foreign State Papers,* 42: 1316. And see also letter from the British consul at Bahia under date of October 23, 1871, contained in *Reports relative to British Consular Establishments,* IV: 103.

*Denmark:* "Should a consular officer in accordance with the laws and regulations of the country, be placed under civil or criminal arrest, the rule is generally followed that his Government receives intimation thereof immediately." *Consular Instructions,* par. 86. Under a circular of 1821, consuls were said to be subject in criminal cases to the same jurisdiction as subjects of the King. Bursotti, I: 163.

*France:* Though arrest for debt was not abolished in France until 1867, consular immunity from such arrest was extended to foreign consuls passing through France on the way to their posts as early as 1840. *Pandects Françaises,* V: 379. The question is now of no practical importance, since imprisonment for debt has been abolished; but see, Elliot, *Diplomatic Code,* II: 511 for arrest of an American consul for debt. When arrest and imprisonment are possible, it is customary first to withdraw the exequatur. *Pandects Françaises,* 21: 379.

*Germany:* " . . . the Law Courts have, I understand, special instructions, according to which certain modified and courteous forms are prescribed to them, in cases where foreign consuls who are foreign functionaries may be implicated or would have to be placed under arrest." *Reports relative to British Consular Establishments,* I: 176.

*Greece:* The instructions of 1834 are peculiar, and it is thought that Greek consuls seeking to act under their provisions would find themselves without the support of any rule of international law. "But, although subject to civil and criminal jurisdiction of the country in which they reside, they can not, however, be arrested, or thrown in prison except for crimes. . . . With regard to crimes and misdemeanors of consuls, which do not offend the public order of the place of their residence, but only the Government of the King, the cognizance belongs to Greek tribunals." Quoted in Bursotti, II: 155. If the term "crimes" is used in the first sentence to exclude misdemeanors, the sentence is not a correct statement of international practice; further, any exemption from civil arrest would depend not upon international practice but upon municipal law in a large number of cases. Just what offenses are embraced in the second quoted sentence is not clear; but if those contemplated included any which when committed by an ordinary individual would serve to give a local court jurisdiction, this provision would not oust that jurisdiction. If offenses are not such as to give a local court jurisdiction, then no exemption from arrest is involved.

*Haiti:* Based on reciprocity, consuls are subject to preliminary arrest only in case of " crimes qualified and punished as such by Haitian laws ". Law of 1912, art. 26.

*Honduras:* Articles 50-52 of the law on foreign consuls are similar to the Mexican law of 1859, *infra.*

*Mexico:* Consuls may not be imprisoned for debt, even in the absence of reciprocal treatment. Law of 1859, art. 18, sec. II.

Arrest for violation of the laws must be made with every consideration compatible with security; facilities must be accorded by the local authorities for the safeguarding of the consular archives and property during the absence of the consul, and for this purpose the officer must be permitted such fredom as is necessary to enable him to place the articles under the consular seal. Nor may authorities seize the opportunity to familiarize themselves with the contents of the archives; their assistance may be rendered only so far as it may be asked. *Ibid.*, art. 28. For an instance of the application of this law, see *Foreign Relations,* 1914: 657.

*Peru: Guía Peruanos,* I: 511.

*Russia:* Under a decree of the Soviet Government consuls may be arrested only after indictment by the Court of the Revolutionary Tribunal.

*Salvador:* Provisions of the law on foreign consuls, arts. 52-55, are similar to the Mexican law of 1859. " They can not be detained or seized for civil cause." Art. 43, sec. 3.

*Venezuela:* The postal laws forbid the sending of money through the mails. In 1912 when the American consul at Maracaibo received two 5-bolivar pieces sent to him through the mails by an American outside of Venezuela with a request that the consul buy kodak films for the remitter, the postmaster informed the consul that he was liable to a fine of 500 bolivars or six weeks' imprisonment. In view of the number of letters from Americans enclosing small coins for the purchase of postage stamps the consul sought to ascertain the extent of his liability, if any. The matter was referred to the postoffice department, which replied that under the postal union Venezuela was within its rights, but pointed out that the law in question seemed to apply only against the remitter, not against the recipient. The matter seems to have been dropped.

*United States:* " It is probable, if he does not engage in business and does not own real estate, that he would not be subject to arrest or incarceration except on a criminal charge; in the case of the commission of a crime he may either be punished by the local laws or sent back to his own country." *Consular Regulations,* 1881, sec. 77; 1888, sec. 50; 1896, sec. 73.

" In the application of the general rules of law to offenses committed by consuls, nothing is better settled by the practice of all the states of Christendom than the doctrine that consuls are subject to criminal process for violation of municipal laws. A foreign consul therefore has no just cause for complaint if, when charged with an offense, he is held amenable to the criminal jurisdiction of the United States ". *Consular Regulations,* 1868, sec. 18.

Under date of July 5, 1911 in reply to an inquiry from a Massachusetts magistrate before whom a Portuguese consul claimed immunity from criminal prosecution, the Secretary of State referred to In re Iasigi, 79 Fed. 751 on the general question of jurisdiction.

When the prosecuting attorney of Fairfield, Conn., sought information regarding applicable treaty provisions in the case of an Italian consul arrested for violation of the speed laws, the Secretary of State under date of May 29, 1923 referred to the treaty of 1878; the effect of the reply seems to be to recognize the liability of the consul.

During the American civil war the United States consul general in Canada was arrested on what was claimed to be a trumped-up charge of false imprisonment. Secretary of State Seward expressly disclaimed any exemption of the consul general from arrest. For the documents relative to the incident, see House Executive Document, No. 39, 38th Congress, 1st session.

See *supra,* page 28 for the imprisonment of an American consul in France, and page 29 for criminal liability of consuls in the United States.

In connection with the arrest of the consular agent at Parral, Mexico, on a charge of passing counterfeit money, the Secretary of State wrote on April 7, 1914:

> The arrest of a consular officer on a criminal charge of passing counterfeit money would appear to be an interference with the performance of the consular duties of the officer, inconsistent with national comity, which it is not believed General Carranza would sanction. You are therefore instructed to bring this matter to his attention at once, and suggest to him the advisability of first submitting to this Government for investigation any infractions of law which may be lodged against its consular officers. You will also say to him that it is the desire of this Government that any further action be suspended in the case of the consular agent at Parral until the charges can be investigated.

It is to be noted that the Secretary of State did not make any of his requests on the basis of international law, but of comity. His suggestion of the advisability of the American government first investigating charges against its consuls is open to very serious question, and probably would not have been made except for the unsettled condition of affairs in Mexico at the time. *Foreign Relations,* 1914, 657.

Treaties carrying provisions for the arrest and punishment of consuls fall into two major groups. One group, beginning with a treaty with Great Britain in 1794 and ending with a treaty with the Orange Free State in 1871, emphasizes the consul's subjection to local laws and states that he may be punished for the violation of those laws. Not a single consular convention falls in this group. The second and more modern group begins with the French consular convention of 1853 and grants to the consul a varying exemption from arrest. The consul's subjection to the ordinary operations of the law is a fundamental assumption of the treaties in this class; protection of the consular function by a limitation of the right to arrest is the design. Variations within the groups are indicated by the summaries:

I. 1. In case of illegal or improper conduct towards the laws or Government, consul may be punished according to law, if the laws will reach the case, or be dismissed, or sent back, the offended Government assigning to other their reasons for the same.

Great Britain, AC&N, 1794: XVI; C&N, 1815: IV.
Sweden and Norway, A&C, 1816: V.

2. In case of illegal or improper conduct with respect to the laws or Government of the country, consul may be prosecuted and punished conformably to the laws and deprived of the exercise of their functions by the offended Government, which shall acquaint the other with their motives.

Greece, C&N, 1837: XII.
Sweden and Norway, C&N, 1824: XIII.

3. In case of offense against the laws, consul may either be punished according to law or sent back, offended Government assigning to the other its reason for same.

Portugal, C&N, 1840: X.

4. In case of offense against the laws, the offended Government may, according to circumstances withdraw his exequatur, send him away from the country, or have him punished in conformity with the laws, assigning to the other Government its reasons for so doing.

Switzerland, FA&E, 1850: VII.

Orange Free State, FC&E, 1871: V.

5. Consuls shall not be arrested, nor shall any of their household be arrested, but their persons and property and houses shall be inviolate. If consul commits any offense against laws of the kingdom, complaint shall be made to the President who will immediately replace the offending officer.

Muscat, A&C, 1833: IX, XVII (adopted by Zanzibar, AC&N, 1886: II).

II. 6. Consuls shall enjoy personal immunity except in case of crimes.

France, CC, 1853: II.

7. Consuls shall be exempt from arrest except in the case of offenses which the local legislation qualifies as crimes and punishes as such.

Belgium, CC, 1868: III.

Italy, CC, 1868: III.

Salvador, AC&CP, 1870: XXXV.

Sweden, CC, 1910: III.

8. Consuls shall enjoy personal immunity except for acts regarded as crimes by the laws of the country in which they reside.

Austria-Hungary, CC, 1870: II.[1]

9. Consuls shall enjoy personal immunity from arrest or imprisonment except in the case of crimes.

German Empire, CC, 1871: III.[2]

10. Consuls shall enjoy personal immunity from arrest or imprisonment except for acts constituting crimes or misdemeanors by the laws of the country in which they reside.

Netherlands, CC, 1878: III.

Spain, F&GR, 1902: XV.

11. Consuls are exempt from arrest or imprisonment in civil cases and from preliminary arrest in penal cases, except in

[1] This clause does not exempt a consular officer from a civil suit for indebtedness. Moore, *Digest*, V: 63.

[2] For an application, see Moore, *Digest*, V: 81-82.

cases of offenses which the local legislation qualifies as crimes and punishes as such.

Italy, CC, 1878: III.

12. Consuls are exempt from preliminary arrest except in the case of offenses which the local legislation qualifies as crimes and punishes as such.

Belgium, CC, 1880: III.
Roumania, CC, 1881: III.
Servia, CC, 1881: III.
Congo, AC&N, 1891: V.
Greece, CC, 1902: III.

13. Consular officers shall be exempt from arrest, except when charged with the commission of offenses locally designated as crimes other than misdemeanors and subjecting the individual guilty thereof to punishment.

Germany, FC&CR, 1923, XVIII.

With regard to the first group of treaties it is only necessary to note that they did not alter the status of the consul as fixed in international law. The consul is liable to arrest for violation of the local laws; the government which has received him may send him out of its territories for such violation. This is the situation in the absence of treaty; and the first group of treaties did not attempt to make any change. The provision that the offended government should assign to the other the reasons for its action is the only modification of the situation in the absence of treaty for the benefit of the sending government.

While the treaties of the second group have as the basis for their provisions the consul's liability to arrest in the territory of the state in which he is functioning, their purpose is to mitigate the rigor of the rule. In all of the treaties of the second group there is an exemption from civil arrest. The exemption from penal arrest varies. In three treaties misdemeanors are mentioned; the others refer only to crimes.

Although the term "crime" is sometimes used to refer to all offenses constituting a violation of the laws, the word is also frequently employed to designate offenses of a major character. It is probable that the proper construction of those provisions exempting consuls from arrest except for offenses locally designated as crimes and punished as such is that the consul is exempt from arrest for the commission of a misdemeanor. Two treaties, however, specifically state that the exemption does not extend to misdemeanors. The latest expression on the subject is the treaty with Germany in 1923; under that convention the exemption from arrest in cases of misdemeanors is expressly granted.

This latter would seem to be the better rule. Though it may be inadvisable to restrict the territorial state's right of jurisdiction to the point of giving exemption from arrest in case of crimes, that objection is not so strong in case of offenses fairly to be designated as misdemeanors. If the offense is not of sufficient gravity to amount to more than a misdemeanor, it would seem that it is hardly of sufficient seriousness to warrant an interruption of the consular business. In the balancing of the interests of the two states the uninterrupted continuance of the consular business would seem to outweigh the necessity for an immediate punishment of an infraction of a minor nature. At any rate this is the latest pronouncement of the Department of State; the insertion of such a provision for the first time at this date indicates that there must be some substantial reason for it. Of course, the receiving state has its protection against abuse of this privilege by the consul in its right to withdraw the consul's exequatur.

# CHAPTER VI

## MISCELLANEOUS

### *Military Billeting and Service*

ANY system of consular immunities designed to give to the consul the freedom necessary for the discharge of the consular functions clearly must have as one of its tenets the protection of the officer from service in the military forces of the state in which he is resident. One of the most widely recognized immunities of consuls is that from such service. While the statements of this immunity vary, it is generally understood that all types of military service, whether in the army, navy, or militia, are included.

An immunity closely allied to that of exemption from military service is that of exemption from military billeting. While the activities of the consul would not be curtailed quite as much by the presence of troops in his house as they would be by his service in the army, the obstacles in the way of the efficient conduct of the consular business imposed by military billeting are sufficient to justify clearly the well-recognized exemption of the consul in this respect. Nor may the consul be required to pay a tax as the alternative of having troops quartered in his house or office.[1]

[1] The following citations are not meant to be exhaustive:

*Belgium: Reports relative to British Establishments,* I: 22 (Antwerp); MS. Department of State, Belgium 21, Document 220 (note of May 19, 1836); *British and Foreign State Papers,* 47: 991 (containing decree of Jan. 1, 1856, art. ii).

*Bolivia:* Regulations, 1887, art. 99.

*Brazil: Reports relative to British Consular Establishments,* IV: 137 (Santos), 143 (Rio de Janeiro).

The exemption from military service is extended to all public service by specific decree in certain states.[1]

Immunity from military billeting and service was accorded in the consular convention with France in 1788, and it has been inserted in practically every consular convention entered into since that time, though in few other treaties.

*France: Foreign Relations*, 1871, p. 272; *Reports relative to British Consular Establishments*, I: 74 (Bordeaux), 63 (Boulogne), 111 (Cherbourg), 124 (Havre); *Pandects Françaises*, vol. 21, pp. 379, 380, nos. 103, 104.

*Germany: Reports relative to British Consular Establishments*, I: 176 (Dantzig).

*Honduras:* Law on Foreign Consuls, art. 41, secs. 2, 3.

*Italy: Reports relative to British Consular Establishments*, I: 221 (Turin).

*Mexico:* Law of 1859, art. 18, pars. 3, 6, and 7; Regulations 1923, art. 53F.

*Netherlands: Consular Instructions*, 1902, p. 37.

*Salvador:* Law on Foreign Consuls, art. 43, secs. 5 and 6.

*Spain:* Wertheim, I: 285; Bursotti, I: 208; *Reports relative to British Consular Establishments*, II: 160 (Barcelona), 210 (Canary Islands), 218 (Porto Rico).

*United States: Consular Regulations*, 1896, sec. 73; 1888, sec. 50; 1881, sec. 77; 1868, sec. 10; *Reports relative to British Consular Establishments*, IV: 10 (Boston).

[1] *Belgium: British and Foreign State Papers*, 47: 991; *Foreign Relations*, 1887, pp. 26-29.

*Denmark: Consular Instructions*, par. 86.

*France: Pandects Françaises*, vol. 21, p. 379, no. 106.

*Germany:* Bursotti, II: 515.

*Honduras:* Law on Foreign Consuls, art. 41, sec. 4.

*Italy: Reports relative to British Consular Establishments*, I: 221 (Turin).

*Mexico:* Law of 1859, art. 18, par. 8.

*Russia: Reports relative to British Consular Establishments*, II: 126 (Taganrog).

*Spain: Ibid.*, II, p. 218 (Porto Rico).

*Venezuela:* Consular Regulations, 1905, art. 31; 1887, art. 33.

*United States: Consular Regulations*, 1896, sec. 73; 1888, sec. 50; 1881, sec. 77; 1870, sec. 22; *Reports relative to British Consular Establishments*, IV: 10 (Boston).

Although military billeting and service are not necessarily inseparable, in only two cases have provisions been made for military billeting without military service, and never has there occurred the exemption from service without that from billeting. The types of exemption are:

1. From military billetings.
   Netherlands, CC, 1855: XIII.
   Spain, F&GR, 1902, XV.
2. From soldiers' billets, militia, watch, guard, guardianship, trusteeship.
   France, CC, 1788: II.
3. From military billetings, service in the militia or the national guard, and other duties of the same nature.
   France, CC, 1853: II.
   Austria-Hungary, 1870: II.
4. From military billetings and contributions, from military service of every sort.
   Germany, CC, 1871: III.
5. From military billetings, service in the militia, national guard, or regular army.
   Belgium, CC, 1868: III.
   Italy, CC, 1868: III.
6. From military billetings, and service in army, navy or militia.
   Congo, AC&N, 1891: V.
7. From military billetings, and from the performance of service in the army, militia, national guard, and navy.
   Italy, CC, 1878: III.
   Netherlands, CC, 1878: III.
   Belgium, CC, 1880: III.
   Roumania, CC, 1881: III.
   Servia, CC, 1881: III.
   Greece, CC, 1902: III.
   Sweden, CC, 1910: III.
8. From military billetings and from service of any military or naval administrative or police character whatsoever.
   Germany, AC&CR, 1923: XVIII.

The exemption from military service was extended to all public service by treaties with France,[1] Colombia,[2] Central America,[3] Brazil,[4] Mexico,[5] Denmark,[6] Chile,[7] Peru-Bolivia,[8] Guatemala,[9] Salvador,[10] Peru, [11] and the German Empire.[12]

### *Communication with Receiving Government*

A consideration of the matter of the consul's right to communicate with the authorities, either central or local, of the state in which he resides shows a two-fold aspect. With whom may the consul communicate and for what purpose? As has been shown before the consul has no diplomatic character; and from this it follows that he does not possess normally the right to communicate with the central authorities of the state within which he is performing his functions. On the other hand, it is imperative at times that the consul have the right to invoke the aid and assistance of the local authorities in his behalf; and it is equally necessary that he be able to communicate with the same authorities when he finds that certain rights of his nationals, which rights he is supposed to protect, have been infringed. Generally, it may be said that a consul does not have the right to communicate with the central authorities of the state which

[1] 1788: CC, II.

[2] 1824: AC&N, XXVIII; 1846 PAN&C, XXXII; 1850: CC, V.

[3] 1825: PAC&N, XXX.

[4] 1826: FC&N, X.

[5] 1831: AC&N, XXIX.

[6] 1826: FC&N, X.

[7] 1832: PAC&N, XXVIII.

[8] 1836: PFC&N, XXVII.

[9] 1849: PFC&N, XXX.

[10] 1850: AN&C, XXXII; and 1870: AC&CP, XXXV.

[11] 1851: FC&N, XXXVI; 1870: FC&N, XXXIII; and 1887: FC&N, XXXI.

[12] 1871: CC, III.

has received him, except where he has been unable to secure justice from the local authorities and there is no diplomatic mission of his state through which he may apply to the proper central authorities for his remedies. In addition to this it is sometimes said that there must be a necessity for immediate action before the consul may resort to the central authorities, even in cases just mentioned. The right to communicate with the local authorities, however, is considerably broader; and it may be said that generally speaking a consul has the right to consult the local authorities whenever such communication is necessary in the course of his duties. More particularly consuls may communicate with the local authorities in cases where there has been an infraction of a treaty between the two states,[1] where an injustice has been done to a fellow national, and where the protection or aid of the local authorities is deemed necessary.

It is believed that the statement of Secretary Olney in 1895 is correct as a statement of international law. There had been some correspondence between the American and Spanish Governments relative to the approach of an Amer-

[1] A limitation of this right is indicated in an article by Dr. Carlos Alfredo Becú, Secretary of the Argentine delegation at the Hague Conferences, published in the *Anuario* for 1908. After stating that consuls may not, with certain exceptions, maintain direct relations with the authorities of the state, Dr. Becú cites a commercial treaty giving the right to communicate in certain cases, notably, succession, arrest and detention of deserters, salvage, and violation of treaties. "Consular officers are restricted, as we have seen, to the protection of commerce and their nationals. Consequently, they may protest only to the violation of treaties which refer to these matters. More particularly, they can only protest against the violation of the faculties and attributions which these treaties concede to them, that is to say, in succession, salvages, apprehension of deserters, etc. Moreover, they may protest against the violation of the immunities and privileges which the same treaties concede to them. This interpretation is not only exact, it is the only possible one. Any other consular attribution with respect to treaties would be equivalent to converting the consul into a diplomatic agent, and this is beyond discussion." Pages 291-294.

ican consul in Cuba to the governor-general of that island. In the course of the correspondence the Secretary wrote: "The governor-general appears to confound the legitimate representation of consular agents when the rights of their countrymen may be assailed with the diplomatic action of an accredited envoy. If so, he clearly forgets that diplomatic relations can only take place directly between sovereigns, and that this government could not by any channel, even through you as the envoy of Spain, or through its own envoy at Madrid, address the governor-general of the island of Cuba as a sovereign authority. It is simply as the local depository and delegate of the sovereign power that the consul addresses him, and then only for the purpose and to the extent fixed by usage as defined in the Spanish-German treaty.[1] Such correspondence is not and can not be diplomatic in any sense. Its object is to furnish a ready and convenient method of adjusting questions at issue on the spot, thereby averting resort to those necessary diplomatic channels which the intercourse of sovereign powers provides." In a later note during the same controversy the Secretary of State wrote:

This statement (of the Spanish Government) would seem to imply a limitation of the subjects upon which a consular representative may properly correspond with the local Spanish authority in Cuba but neither is such limitation expressly confirmed by you nor can it be fairly inferred from the text of the treaty between Spain and Germany, in which I find the fullest conventional definition of the right, or from precedent and usage. The right of consuls "to address the authorities of their districts in remonstrance against every infraction of the treaties and conventions existing between the two countries and against whatever abuse may be claimed by their country-

[1] This treaty was applicable by virtue of the most-favored-nation clause in a treaty of 1870 between Spain and the United States.

men" clearly includes initial representation upon those subjects. It may indeed happen that the precise form of remedy may have to be referred to His Majesty's Government and that appropriate redress may be obtainable only after diplomatic negotiations between the two Governments.

But such negotiations are the sequel of the original remonstrance and are made necessary only when and because the local authorities show themselves lacking either in the will or power to adequately deal with the grievance. This is clearly expressed in the concluding paragraph of Article IX of the Spanish-German treaty of February 22, 1870, which specifically authorizes consuls, in the absence of the diplomatic agent of their country, to conduct such further diplomatic discussion with the supreme government, thus clearly distinguishing between the incident in its incipient stage and the incident when it has passed that stage and become a subject of diplomatic treatment.

Nevertheless, though the subject treated of may ultimately become the theme of diplomatic negotiations, that circumstance cannot deprive the consul of the clear right nor absolve him from the clear duty of initiating such inquiries and remonstrances as the interests intrusted to his keeping may from time to time require. (*Foreign Relations*, 1895, pp. 1209-1214.)

While the Secretary of State had before him an applicable treaty provision, it is clear that his understanding of the situation was that the statement made by him was a correct statement of the relation of the consul to the local authorities even in the absence of a treaty.[1]

[1] A few consular regulations merely state that consuls do not have the right to address themselves to the authorities of the place where they function. It would seem that this refers to the central, not the local, authorities; thus:

*Bolivia:* Regulations of 1877, art. 20.
*Chile:* Regulations, 1860, art. 15.
*Costa Rica:* Regulations, 1888, art. 17.
*Ecuador:* Regulations, 1870, art. 15.
*Honduras:* Regulations, 1906, art. 20.
*Salvador:* Regulations, 1905, art. 91.

A peculiar situation is possible where rebels are in control

The usual statement is one which corresponds to that in the text—that consuls have the right to consult the central authorities in the absence of a representative of the legation; this, however, only after recourse to the local authorities has failed to give satisfaction. The following regulations are typical:

*Argentina:* Regulations, 1906, art. 59.

*Bolivia:* Regulations, 1887, art. 22.

*Brazil: British and Foreign State Papers,* vol. 42, p. 1316.

*Colombia: Guía Consular,* p. 29; Palau, *Guía,* p. 6; Law of 1866, art. 38.

*Denmark: Consular Instructions,* par. 24.

*Ecuador:* Decree of Oct. 27, 1916 contained in *Leyes,* etc., 1917.

*Germany: General Instructions,* 1872, p. 10.

*Honduras:* Law on Foreign Consuls, art. 16.

*Mexico: Derecho Internacional,* III: 182; Regulations 1923, arts. 17, 18 and 53C; Regulations, 1911, arts. 47, 198, 199; Law of 1859, art. 33, sec. 3 and art. 10, sec. 10.

*Panama: Leyes y Decretos,* 1916, art. 36.

*Peru: Guía Peruanos,* I: 556; Regulations, 1863, arts. 10 and 11.

*Russia: Reports relative to British Consular Establishments,* II: 116.

*Salvador:* Law on Foreign Consuls, arts. 13 and 51.

*Spain: Reports relative to British Consular Establishments,* II: 160, 218.

*Sweden: Consular Ordinance and Instructions,* Rules 45 and 56.

*Switzerland: Regulations,* art. 28, sec. 5.

*Uruguay:* Regulations, 1917, arts. 19, 58; 1906, arts. 21 and 73; 1878, art. 132; see also 1917, p. 50.

*Venezuela:* Regulations, 1923, art. 30; 1921, art. 24; 1910, art. 42; 1905, art. 36; Decree of June 27, 1912 in *Gaceta Oficial,* June 28, 1912.

*United States:* General Instructions, 1833, art. 16; 1855, secs. 15 and 16; Regulations, 1868, secs. 10, 30 and 31; 1881, secs. 77 and 426; 1888, secs. 50 and 398; 1896, secs. 73 and 437. The latest expression of the privilege in an American treaty (that of friendship, commerce and consular rights with Germany, 1923, article XXI) is as follows:

"Consular officers, nationals of the state by which they are appointed may, within their respective consular districts, address the authorities, national, state, provincial, or municipal, for the purpose of protecting their countrymen in the enjoyment of their rights accruing by treaty or otherwise. Complaint may be made for the infraction of those rights. Failure upon the part of the proper authorities to grant redress or to accord protection may justify interposition through the diplomatic channel, and in the absence of a diplomatic representative a consul general or the other consular officer stationed at the capital may apply directly to the government of the country."

of the territory within which is included the consular district. This was the situation in which British consuls in the southern states found themselves during the American civil war. The action of the British consul in Charleston in communicating with the Confederate Government, under instructions from his own Government, led to a sharp protest by the United States Government, and the revocation of the consul's exequatur. Earl Russell pointed out the futility of the British Government's consulting the Government at Washington with regard to the conduct of the Confederate Government within the area under the latter's control. The Secretary of State, while recognizing the validity of Earl Russell's statement, pointed out that the United States could hardly be expected to permit a consul to whom it had given an exequatur to carry on communications which might tend to undermine the authority of the United States. *Foreign Relations,* 1862, pp. 1-9.[1]

### *Respect Due to Consuls* [2]

In addition to the above more or less tangible privileges and immunities which the consul may claim, many states recognize as due him a certain "honor" and "respect" Thus in Venezuela foreign consuls must be treated and considered with the honor and respect which is due to persons who have the confidence of the government which names them and that which admits them; further they are to be given seat and place with the municipal authorities of the city in which they reside in the order of their relative seniority upon public occasions. Decree of January 15, 1883, art. 5, contained in Seijas, I: 432, 433.

[1] See Hall, *Int. Law,* note to section 105 for a criticism.

[2] Hyde, *Int. Law,* I: 795-796 contains an excellent brief description of this respect as observed by the United States, based upon laws, cases, and diplomatic pronouncements.

This honor and respect most certainly is sufficient to protect the consul from personal violence on the part of the local authorities. Thus, when the British vice consul at San Jose, Guatemala was arrested for declining to enter the house of the *comandante* when requested to do so, and subsequent to his arrest was mistreated, the Guatemalan Government was compelled to indemnify the consul and to salute the British flag. *Foreign Relations,* 1874, pp. 154-163; *British State Papers,* 1875, pp. 875-922; Stowell, E. C., *The Magee Incident.*

The Honduranean and Salvadorean laws governing foreign consuls specifically provide that " As a rule, the authorities must protect foreign consuls, and they will employ the means at their disposal to guarantee to them the full exercise of their functions." Arts. 40 and 42 respectively.

The Brazilian imperial decree of 1831 instructed Brazilian officers who found it necessary to enter a consulate to observe " due deference ". *British and Foreign State Papers,* 42: 1316.

A further instance of this special treatment of consuls is witnessed by the action of the Czechoslovakian Government in exempting consular vehicles from the mobilization law of 1924, which provides that the Government may seize during mobilization and in time of war all private means of transportation. Chargé to Secretary of State, July 24, 1924.

In the absence of the American vice consul at Rouen, French secret service agents entered his home and questioned his servants in 1915. Upon the return of the vice consul, he immediately filed a protest and representatives of the military authorities called upon him expressing their regrets and stating that they were not aware of the position of the vice consul. Ambassador at Paris to Secretary of State, April 13, 1915.

The Mexican Government lists first among those immunities which consuls may claim under international law the "right of protection of person of consul". Regulations, 1923, art. 53A.

In 1911 a group of Mexican rebels stood in front of the Mexican consulate in Douglas, Arizona, and insulted the personnel of the office whenever they came out on the street. The Department of State immediately requested the governor of Arizona to investigate and take appropriate action. *Foreign Relations,* 1911, p. 481.

So important does the United States consider this respect due the consul that a provision regarding it was inserted in the 1923 treaty of friendship, commerce, and consular rights with Germany, article XVII of which provides that "As official agents, such officials, shall be entitled to the high consideration of all officials, national or local, with whom they have official intercourse in the state which receives them".

The position of the United States in the absence of treaty is well summarized in Hyde's *International Law* (vol. I, pp. 795-796), the following statement being amply supported by the authorities there cited:

The yielding of consular privileges and immunities is for the purpose of facilitating the performance of the consular function. Such performance is retarded unless respect for that function be maintained and contempt for it both prevented and penalized. Respect is enhanced by provisions in numerous conventions of the United States conferring upon a consul special privileges, such as, for example, that of giving his testimony in a civil case, at his consulate rather than in open court. The consular function is upheld in the United States by the Federal law punishing one who falsely assumes or pretends to be a consular officer of a foreign government duly accredited as such to the Government of the United States, with intent to defraud such government or any person, and takes upon himself to act as such officer, or in such pretended character demands or obtains, or attempts to obtain from any person or from such foreign government, or from any officer thereof, any money, paper, document, or other thing of value. It is doubtless also possible to enjoin one who interferes with or obstructs the performance by a consul of his official duties.[1]

In their intercourse with local or minor officials oftentimes ignorant of the law of nations and of the terms of existing conventions, consular officers are not infrequently subjected to humiliation, and occasionally to insult. When a foreign consular officer within the United States is the victim of such treatment, there appears to be no law which subjects the offender to prosecution in the Federal courts. Frank expression of regret is, nevertheless, to be anticipated upon reasonable protest duly lodged with the superior authorities, State or Federal. If, because of the absence of appropriate statute or for any other reason, the State authorities are unable or indisposed to inflict any penalty upon the offender, the country to which the consul belongs may justly seek redress through the diplomatic channel.

### *Respect Due from Consuls*

Although consuls occupy a privileged position, this does not extend to an interference in local affairs. Inevitably these officers in the discharge of their functions are thrown

[1] In a note to this sentence, the author states:

"If the consul be an alien, it is believed that he may rely upon paragraph 17, section 24, Chap. 2, of the Federal Judicial Code of Mar. 3, 1911, conferring original jurisdiction upon the United States District Courts, 'of all suits brought by any alien for a tort only, in violation of the laws of nations or of a treaty of the United States'. Interference with the performance of the consular functions of one empowered to exercise the same by the State to which he is appointed as well as by his own country, violates the law of nations, and in most instances, also, the provisions of treaties which the consular officer may justly invoke.

"See, also, Act No. 51 of April 15, 1913, Pennsylvania Sess. Laws of 1913, making it under certain circumstances unlawful for any person, firm or corporation to use the word 'Consul' or 'Consulate', or the coat of arms of a foreign country for exhibition, display, or advertising purposes, and providing a penalty therefor."

into contact with the authorities and people of the state within which they reside. In the interests of efficient conduct of the consular business, consuls are regularly forbidden by their own governments to participate in local politics. This holds both in time of peace and in time of war.[1]

[1] *Argentina:* Regulations, 1906, arts. 61, 67, 68.
*Bolivia:* Regulations, 1887, art. 23.
*Chile:* Regulations, 1915, art. 119; 1897, art. 53.
*Colombia: Guía Consular,* pp. 10, 29; *Manual Consular Colombiano,* pp. 28, 157, 173.
*Costa Rica:* Regulations, 1888, art. 246.
*Cuba: Instrucciones Provisionales,* p. 7.
*Denmark:* Instructions, pars. 8, 23.
*Ecuador:* Circular No. 12, of May 15, 1902, contained in *Ley y Decretos,* etc., 1909, p. 77; Regulations, 1870, art. 62.
*Germany: General Instructions,* p. 10.
*Greece:* Instructions of 1834, art. 12.
*Guatemala: Derecho Patrio,* pp. 245, 246.
*Hawaii:* Regulations, 1895, art. 5; 1880, art. 3.
*Honduras:* Regulations, 1906, arts. 39, 40.
*Liberia:* Regulations, art. 29.
*Mexico:* Regulations, 1923, art. 18; 1871, art. 14; Law of 1859, arts. 11, 12 and 14.
*Netherlands:* Consular Regulations, ch. i, pars. 6, 10; 1902, art. 5.
*Nicaragua:* Regulations, 1880, arts. 14, 15, 17, 18.
*Paraguay:* Regulations, 1871, arts. 37, 53.
*Peru:* Regulations, 1897, arts. 31, 32, 40; 1888, arts. 42-44, 57; 1863, arts. 3, 4, 7.
*Salvador:* Regulations, 1905, art. 137.
*South Africa:* Regulations, art. 4.
*Sweden: Consular Ordinance and Instructions,* art. 30, rules 32 and 45.
*Texas:* Regulations, arts. 45, 46.
*Uruguay:* Regulations, 1917, arts. 60-62; 1906, arts. 76, 77; 1878, art. 41.
*Venezuela:* Regulations, 1923, art. 29; 1921, art. 23; 1910, art. 27; 1905, arts. 37, 38; 1887, arts. 40, 41; Consular Law, 1885, art. 37; Consular Law, 1865, art. 21.
*United States:* Instructions, 1833, arts. 45, 46. Secretary Livingston in these instructions specifically refers to the "disturbed and unsettled conditions of the republics of South America and United Mexican States". *General Instructions,* 1855, secs. 10, 11; Regulations, 1868, secs. 20, 21, 28; 1870, secs. 300-304; 1881, secs. 426-429; 1888, secs. 398-400; 1896, secs. 438-439.

A violation of the rule is held to be sufficient grounds to warrant the receiving state in withdrawing the exequatur of the offending consul. Thus in 1881 the exequatur of the British vice consul at Ciudad Bolivar was withdrawn for participation in local politics. The offense seems to have been in misrepresenting certain acts of the Government in order to assist a revolution. *Memoria de Relaciones Esteriores,* 1881 (Venezuela), quoted in Seijas, I: 465-470.

*British and Foreign State Papers,* 48: 189-300 contain correspondence relative to the withdrawal of a British consul's exequatur for alleged violation of the American neutrality act. In 1894 the Colombian Government requested the Salvadorean Government to withdraw its consul at Bogota for mixing in politics and publishing a paper in which acts of the Government were censured and attacked. The request was immediately complied with. Uribe, IV: 663.

Action of the British consul in Abyssinia in aligning himself with one of the factions in a struggle for the local throne met with censure from the Foreign Office. *British and Foreign State Papers,* 53: 51.

A person claiming to be the Austro-Hungarian vice consul at Richmond, Virginia, was the editor of a paper styled "The Crucible". While the paper purported to serve the purpose of promoting a better understanding of the German people by the United States, much of it was devoted to attacks on the administration for its action in permitting the sale of munitions by American citizens to the British Government. Investigation proved that the individual in question had not been recognized as a consular officer by the American Government. The record is sufficient to indicate that had he been so recognized, his exequatur would have been withdrawn immediately. Secretary of State to Austro-Hungarian Ambassador, April 7, 1915.

During the period before the American entry into the world war there were a number of instances of participation by German consuls in acts contrary to laws of the United States in an attempt to prevent American aid from reaching the allies. Such acts were a part of a general plan fostered by German diplomatic officers in the United States; and consular participation received a share of the condemnation visited upon the whole course of conduct.[1]

These cases are to be distinguished from those where the consul intercedes with the local authorities in behalf of measures for the benefit of his fellow nationals. In this respect the consul is not under the same handicap as a diplomatic officer; and instances of a consul appearing before a state legislative committee are not unknown. Such a practice does not seem to have incurred the displeasure of either the national or state governments in the United States. Article XXI of the 1923 treaty with Germany seems broad enough to establish this as a right of the consul.

### *Consular Speeches and Writings*

Closely allied to the above consideration of the relation of the consul to the politics of the state in which he is situated are the regulations which prevent consuls from alluding in public speeches to matters of controversy which may be pending between the state they represent and the one in which they reside. This prohibition even goes so far as a recommendation that the consul refrain from all public speeches; and when public addresses are deemed essential, they are assumed to be entirely innocuous, containing nothing which might incite feelings against the government which the consul represents or which could be construed to

[1] See *German Plots and Intrigues in the United States During the Period of Our Neutrality*, a pamphlet issued by the Committee on Public Information, July, 1918, Red, White and Blue Series, No. 10.

constitute a taking of sides in local political controversies. Furthermore, consuls are not permitted by most states to publish any articles or books which would contain material of the sort not permitted in speeches.[1]

### *Acceptance of Decorations and Gifts*

Several states have provided that consuls may not accept from the government or from the authorities of the district any decoration, present, emolument, public charge, or title of any nature; though in some cases, permission may be granted by the proper authorities of the state appointing the officer.[2]

[1] *Bolivia:* Regulations, 1887, art. 24.
*Costa Rica:* Regulations, 1888, art. 246.
*Ecuador:* Regulations, 1870, art. 61.
*Greece:* Instructions of 1834, art. 63.
*Honduras:* Regulations, 1906, art. 41.
*Mexico: Guía Diplomática y Consular,* pp. 103, 104; Regulations, 1911, arts. 43, 44.
*Nicaragua:* Regulations, 1880, art. 18.
*Peru:* Regulations, 1863, art. 7.
*Salvador:* Regulations, 1905, art. 136.
*United States:* Regulations, 1868, sec. 29; 1870, sec. 289; 1881, secs. 423, 424; 1888, secs. 395, 396; 1896, secs. 435 and 436. "This prohibition does not extend to literary articles or subjects not connected with politics, but communications to newspapers and their representatives relating to epidemics and diseases abroad are forbidden. Violation of the rule in the articles above set forth led to the issuance of circular instructions No. 595 of April 25, 1918 and No. 612 of August 3, 1918, calling attention to the prohibitions contained therein.

[2] *Bolivia:* Regulations, 1887, art. 25.
*Colombia: Manual Consular Colombiano,* p. 58.
*Germany:* General Instructions, par. 5.
*Greece:* Instructions, 1834, art. 62.
*Netherlands:* Regulations, ch. i, par. 13 and supplement number 8.
*Peru:* Regulations, 1863, art. 8.
*United States:* Regulations, 1922, based on General Instructions No. 298; Regulations, 1896, sec. 451; 1888, sec. 421; 1881, sec. 450; Instructions, 1855, sec. 13. The American provision permits acceptance when authorized by Congress. House Miscellaneous Document No. 189, 42nd

### *Domicile*

It is generally conceded that consuls while resident within the consular district may retain their domicile in the state from which they were sent.[1]

### *Miscellaneous*

When rumors of an attempt to assassinate the American consul at Porfirio Diaz, Mexico, prompted that individual to wire the Department of State for protection, the Secretary of State, Mr. Bryan, sent the following request to the Secretary of War on June 4, 1914: "While it is not desired to send a military force across the line except as a last resort, there would appear to be ample authority and precedent for doing so to prevent the killing of, or injury to, the consular representative of this nation whom the appropriate Mexican authorities are unable to protect. I therefore have the honor to request that you will at once issue the necessary instructions to the officers at Eagle Pass to keep closely in communication with the consul and to hold a force in readiness to go to his aid if the necessity arises."

Consular privileges do not include that of importing liquor for the personal use of the consul into the United States. Requests made by the Siamese consul general for this purpose were refused on Feb. 19, 1920. So also two trunks

Congress, Second Session contains a joint resolution authorizing American consular officers to receive certain testimonials from the German Emperor for services performed in behalf of German citizens during the Franco-Prussian war.

[1] *France:* Letter from French consul general at New Orleans, March 11, 1924.

*Denmark:* Consular Instructions, par. 86.

*Mexico:* Law of 1923, art. 20.

*Peru:* Letter from Peruvian consul general at San Francisco, April 11, 1924.

*United States:* Wheat *v.* Smith (1888) 7 S. W. 161.

addressed to a certain consul general at New York were seized by customs officials at Ogdensburg, New York, on Nov. 4, 1920, because upon examination they were found to contain nothing but liquor.

The Eighteenth Amendment to the United States Constitution contains no exceptions whatever. Diplomatic officers importing liquor have not been prosecuted because of the general immunity from criminal jurisdiction. And as the consul does not share the diplomat's immunity from prosecution, any attempt on his part to import liquors would make him criminally liable.

Freedom of worship was formerly specially conceded to consuls, but today the general position of states relative to freedom of worship is such that provision for it need not be specially made. See Mexican law of 1859, art. 18, sec. 1.

A peculiar situation unlikely to arise again because of the conditions of modern warfare led to the censuring of an American consul in 1868. In that year the consul at Rome asked for and received permission to accompany papal troops going out against Garibaldi. Unexpectedly, he found himself in the zone of fighting, and upon going to the assistance of a wounded officer of the papal troops was soon under fire. After being slightly wounded, he took up the musket of the wounded officer in self-defense. Later he assisted in caring for the wounded of both sides. His action was deemed worthy of censure in that though he could not have foreseen that his going as a spectator would result in his becoming a combatant, yet he impliedly lent his moral support to one of the belligerents in showing that he believed it would be able to protect him, and thus lessened his ability to look after United States interests, especially in the event the Garibaldians were successful.

In reply to inquiries from attorneys designed to ascertain whether the Department of State would assist in the collection of a judgment rendered against an American consul, the Department replied that while it was "very willing to facilitate your communication with any of its consular officers who may be indebted to you, and while any apparent failure of a consular officer to settle his private obligations cannot but bring upon him its grave dissatisfaction, the Department cannot in any event act as an agency for the collection of such debts." Likewise, on Dec. 1, 1911, the Department refused to permit the attachment of the consular salary.

*General Clauses in Treaties*

Three broad provisions supplement those specifically enumerated in American treaties: the most-favored-nation clause, certain general expressions, and a statement of a residual liability. The most important of these in point of frequency of occurrence as well as in extent, is the most-favored-nation clause; and it must be considered in connection with any particular treaty. As it has been inserted in sixty-seven [1] treaties with fifty-one different states, it is

[1] Morocco (1787 and 1836), France (1788 and 1853), Spain (1795 and 1902), Tripoli (1805), Algiers (1815 and 1816), Colombia (1824 and 1846), Central America (1825), Denmark (1826), Brazil (1828), Prussia (1828), Austria-Hungary (1829, 1848 and 1870), Mexico (1831), Russia (1832), Chile (1832), Venezuela (1836 and 1860), Peru-Bolivia (1836), Sardinia (1838), Ecuador (1839), Portugal (1840), Hanover (1840 and 1846), Two Sicilies (1845 and 1855), Mecklenburg-Schwerin (1847), Guatemala (1849), Hawaiian Islands (1849), Switzerland (1850), Salvador (1850), Peru (1851, 1870 and 1887), Costa Rica (1851), Argentine Republic (1853), Netherlands (1855 and 1878), Persia (1856), Bolivia (1858), Paraguay (1859), Honduras (1864), Haiti (1864), Madagascar (1867 and 1881), Nicaragua (1867), Orange Free State (1871), Germany (1871 and 1923), Belgium (1880), Servia (1881), Roumania (1881), Corea (1882), Zanzibar (1886), Tonga (1886), Congo (1891), Japan (1894 and 1911), Greece (1902), China (1903), Sweden (1910) and Siam (1920).

For an interpretation of the most-favored-nation clause with reference to consular treaties see Hyde, *Int. Law*, vol. ii, sec. 537, and Ludwig,

quite possible that a consideration of those exemptions granted in treaties to which the United States is a party may not reveal all of those which a consul of the United States stationed at a particular post may enjoy by virtue of some treaty provision. This enumeration does not include the most-favored-nation clause as found generally in commercial treaties; it extends only to the clause when used with special reference to consular officers. It is very likely, however, that somewhere among the many provisions on the subject of consular privileges all of the more important exemptions have been put into operation by an American treaty; and it is believed that every such provision has been considered.

In addition to the most-favored-nation clause, it is necessary to examine the various general provisions which, appearing from time to time, might be construed to add privileges in some cases. The earliest of these general provisions was contained in the treaty of amity, commerce, and navigation with Great Britain in 1794. No attempt was made to define consular privileges other than this: ". . . the said consuls shall enjoy those liberties and rights which belong to them by reason of their function."

Three years later a similar treaty with Tunis secured to the consul, his family, and his suite, the protection of the government.[1] This was expanded in 1805 in a treaty of peace and amity with Tripoli to:[2]

Ernest, *Consular Treaty Rights.* Hyde observes that the clause when applied with reference to administration of estates by consuls has been assumed by the courts to be unconditional. In cases with reference to fiscal concessions, the clause has been interpreted by the Department of State; and in accordance with the general American interpretation of the most-favored-nation clause has been treated as conditional.

[1] Article XVII.

[2] Article XIV.

The consuls shall have liberty and personal security both by land and sea, and shall not be prevented from going on board any vessel that they may think proper to visit. They shall have likewise the liberty to appoint their own dragoman and broker.

Treaties in 1816 and 1827 with Sweden and Norway provided that the consular officer should enjoy all the protection and assistance necessary for the due discharge of his functions.[1] Practically the same provision is to be found in Article XII of a treaty of commerce and navigation with Greece in 1837. To this grant of protection and assistance, a treaty with the Ottorman Empire [2] added for the only time in the history of American treaties "suitable distinction".

This general provision was followed in the main but was qualified by treaties with the Netherlands [3] and with Belgium,[4] the effective statement in these treaties permitting consular officers to enjoy all the privileges, protection, and assistance usually appertaining to their offices and which were necessary for the proper discharge of their functions; while the French consular convention of 1853 prefaced the immunities set forth by the statement that they were such as were usually accorded to the consular office.[5]

Twice there has been expressed in American treaties the idea which executive regulations have steadily declared—that consuls are not entitled to diplomatic immunities. In statements introducing the prerogatives enumerated in treaties with Colombia [6] and Salvador [7] the contracting states in

[1] 1816, A&C, V; 1827, C&N, XIII.

[2] 1830: C&N, II.

[3] 1839: C&N, II.

[4] CC: V.

[5] Article II.

[6] CC: V.

[7] AC&CP: XXXV.

each instance declined to recognize any diplomatic character of consuls and specifically denied to them the privileges and immunities attaching to diplomatic officers; but to enable consuls to expedite their business, certain prerogatives were granted in the treaties.

The treaty of amity, commerce, and consular privileges with Salvador in 1870 contained the unusual provision that consular officers in everything that exclusively concerned the exercise of their functions, should be independent of the state in whose territory they were residing.[1] This was the same expression found in the consular convention with Colombia (1850: V); otherwise the nearest approach to the position is to be found in a statement in the consular convention with the German Empire to the effect that consular officers should not be interfered with in the exercise of their official functions any further than was necessary for the administration of the laws of the country.[2]

This provision was invoked by the German consul at Cincinnati when a certain person in that city used misleading advertisements and displayed the German flag in such a manner as to leave the impression that he was a German consul. The attorney general was of opinion that the case was not covered by any law of the United States; but when this matter was called to the attention of the local authorities, it was amicably settled.[3]

On the other hand, in many cases it has been specifically provided that the immunities enumerated by treaty are the only ones which the consular officer may claim. The ordinary expression of this idea came in 1824, though it had previously found a place in the French consular convention

[1] Article XXXV.

[2] 1871: III.

[3] Moore, *Digest*, V: 42 (1887); also Hyde, *Int. Law*, I: 796.

of 1788.[1] The provision "being in everything else subject to the laws of the respective states" was included in treaties with Colombia,[2] Central America,[3] Denmark,[4] Brazil,[5] Mexico,[6] Chile,[7] Venezuela,[8] Peru-Bolivia,[9] Ecuador,[10] Guatemala,[11] Salvador,[12] Peru,[13] Netherlands,[14] Bolivia,[15] and Haiti.[16] In many instances, however, this must be read in connection with the most-favored-nation clause. Although these treaties have a common residual clause, it is not to be understood that the residuum is the same in all cases; the immunities granted have been presented in the preceding chapters.

*The Position of the Consul in Time of War*

The effect of the outbreak of war between the state appointing the consul and that which receives him upon the position of the officer has never been very well defined; nor has there been a clear definition of the status of a consul in territory which is a seat of civil war against the government from which the consul received his exequatur. There seems

[1] Article II.
[2] 1824: AC&N, XXVIII; 1846: PAN&C, XXXII; 1850: CC, VI.
[3] 1825: PAC&N, XXX.
[4] 1826: FC&N, X.
[5] 1828: AC&N, XXX.
[6] 1831: AC&N, XXIX.
[7] 1832: PAC&N, XXVIII.
[8] 1836: PAC&N, XXXI.
[9] 1836: PFC&N, XXVII.
[10] 1839: PFN&C, XXXI.
[11] 1849: PFC&N, XXX.
[12] 1850: AC&N, XXXII.
[13] 1851: FC&N, XXXVI; 1870: FC&N, XXXIII; 1887: FC&N, XXXI.
[14] 1855: CC, II.
[15] 1858: PFC&N, XXXIII.
[16] 1864: ACN&E, XXXV.

to be more official material upon the subject of the consul's communication with his own government under these circumstances than upon any other phase of the situation. From the standpoint of the United States, one source of diplomatic problems of this nature arose from the domestic difficulties in Mexico during the period from 1910 to 1920.

Rebel and federal forces alike seemed to find it advisable to limit consular communications, though in both cases the superior authorities disavowed the acts of the petty commanders who enforced the offensive restrictions. In 1912 General Orozco, the rebel commander, refused to recognize consular representatives of the United States in the territory controlled by the rebels, because of the fact that the United States had refused to recognize the existence of a state of belligerency. This action of the general was followed by a seizure of mail addressed to the consul and a delay of telegrams. When on April 17 General Orozco agreed to an informal and unofficial recognition of the consuls, one of the points stipulated as the basis for this recognition was non-interference with mails and the right of consuls to transmit telegrams either open or in cipher without any delay. *Foreign Relations,* 1912, p. 792.

For a considerable period of time American consuls throughout Mexico regularly reported to the Department of State that mails and telegrams were delayed. Thus, on January 27, 1915, the consul at Aguas Calientes reported that telegraphic communication from his post to Mexico City had been closed to the public, though still open to the military authorities. A message from the consul to the Brazilian legation, then representing the interests of the United States, was refused. General Villa promised to reply to a protest made to him by the consul, but no record has been found of such reply having been made. The consul at Frontera likewise reported on April 24, 1914, that "this office is completely isolated as the telegraph office will not accept any telegrams from this consulate; the mail service is also interrupted. Even if the mails should eventually leave this post, it is almost certain that my despatches for the consul general would be violated, if not destroyed."

The Secretary of State took a hand in the matter on August 6, 1915, by wiring to Mr. Carothers at El Paso to request General Villa to issue appropriate orders to secure the opening of telegraph lines to consular messages. This was followed on August 8 by a message from the consul at Chihuahua that telegraph lines were again open to consular messages.

Again on September 2, 1915, the consul at Frontera reported difficulty in having telegrams transmitted. It seems that the telegraph office placed obstacles in the way of the transmission of telegrams, and in reply to a protest informed the consul that the lines were cut. The governor stated that he had no power to order the telegrams to be transmitted, so the office permitted the consul to telegraph General Alvarado for permission to send the messages. The general replied that he had instructed the operator to transmit the telegrams, but the latter again reported that the lines had been cut when the consul made a further attempt to send his report.

After rebels had refused to permit messengers from the consulate at Mazatlan to deliver messages and had violated the consular seal, destroying some messages sent by the consul, General Carranza promised on February 19, 1914, to make an investigation looking to the punishment of those guilty of violating the consular correspondence. The action of the American vice consul at Saltillo on November 6, 1913, in filing a vigorous protest against the refusal of the telegraph company to accept official telegrams was approved by the Department of State. The consular agent at Torreon on April 23, 1914, reported that his telegrams relative to Americans in his consular district were either refused or delayed. *Foreign Relations*, 1914, 672.

A second group of protests from American consuls was hinged on the refusal of various authorities in Mexico to accept code messages unless they were accompanied by a Spanish translation. Among the protests may be included those coming from the consul at Frontera, Feb. 2, 1915, and Feb. 3, 1915; Vera Cruz, March 22, 1915; Durango, April 27, 1914 (*Foreign Relations*, 1914, p. 672); and Chihuahua, August 6, 1915.

The position taken by the Department of State in each of these cases was that the Mexican government had no authority to prohibit code messages; thus, on Feb. 8, 1915, the Department telegraphed, "inform appropriate authorities this government insists upon the right of its consuls to communicate freely with the Department and in code when deemed advisable. Request that suitable instructions be sent telegraph office at Frontera to pass consular code messages."

The vice consul at Durango reported on July 29, 1915, that for the preceding twelve days the authorities had refused to pass any mail addressed to the consul.

The war which began in Europe in 1914 was the occasion of considerable correspondence as to the status of consular communication. On November 9, 1914, the American minister at Athens reported the arrival of a message from the consul at Smyrna with a request that he wire the Department that official mail under seal was refused by the Turkish post-office, whose officials demanded that it be posted open for their inspection. The ambassador at Constantinople was instructed to enter a proper protest.

On November 13, 1914, the ambassador at Berlin reported that the existing German regulations required consular officers of neutral states to leave unsealed their correspondence to foreign countries, including communications to their own government. The ambassador reported that he had called the attention of consuls to the Department's pouch service for the protection of official correspondence. The action of the ambassador was approved on November 17, 1914, and there is nothing to indicate that the Department protested against the German position.

The situation with regard to consular correspondence in Austria-Hungary had become such by November 14 that the ambassador requested instructions covering the point. It seems the censors had opened letters addressed by consuls in Austria-Hungary to diplomatic and consular officers in other states.

In an endeavor to secure a uniform rule governing the treatment of consular correspondence, the Department of State on November 25, 1914, sent identic telegrams to Vienna, London, Berlin, Paris, Bucharest, Rome, and Tokio. The position which the United States desired to have the warring states approve was that: first, all correspondence between American diplomatic and consular officers in the territory of a belligerent should be inviolable if under seal of office; second, no correspondence of private individuals should be forwarded by diplomatic or consular officers under official seal or cover; third, official correspondence between American diplomatic officers residing in different states should not be molested if under seal of office; fourth, official correspondence under seal of office between the Department of State and the American diplomatic and consular officers should not be opened or molested; fifth, pouches under seal between American diplomatic missions sent by mail or by courier should not be opened or molested; sixth, all correspondence other than the above should be sent by ordinary mail, subject to usual censorship.

The replies were as follows: Austria-Hungary agreed. Russia stated that the correspondence was already exempted by decree of August 2 concerning the temporary military censorship. Germany was willing to exempt communication from the ambassador to the consul and *vice versa,* but not letters between consuls nor letters from a consul to a government other than his own. Communication from the Department to the embassy and to consulates was exempted from censorship and from the embassy to the Department, but from the consulate to the Department only when sent through the embassy. Japan thought the agreement was unnecessary, but was willing to enter into it on condition that the communication should be sent by pouch. France stated that no diplomatic or consular correspondence had been opened up until that time, and that while reserving the principle involved, she was willing to maintain the inviolability of diplomatic correspondence and, "actuated by friendly spirit", that of consular agents. Servia agreed. Turkey indicated that the gravity of the situation forbade any change in the existing regulations, which authorized military commanders of districts where military movement was taking place to stop all sealed official correspondence between consulates and the embassy.

On April 23, 1915, the Department of State addressed the following telegraphic communication to its diplomatic representatives:

In view of understanding between United States and belligerent countries regarding inviolability of Department's diplomatic and consular correspondence, the following rules established by the Department are hereby called to your attention:

1. Communications from private individuals or institutions abroad to private individuals or institutions in United States should not be sent in Department pouches.

2. Personal letters from United States diplomatic or consular

officers or employees of American missions or consulates abroad addressed to private individuals in the United States may be sent in pouches, but should be censored by heads of missions with a view to prevent transmission of statements which would otherwise be censored by Governments, and should be left unsealed with postage fully prepaid.

3. Official correspondence of diplomatic and consular officers to individuals outside of the Department should be marked "Official Business" and should be left unsealed.

4. Communications from nations at war to agents in the United States should not be transmitted through pouches.

5. The Department reserves right to censor all mail received in the pouches.

On November 23, 1914, the Turkish Government issued instructions to the effect that while cipher telegrams might not be exchanged between consulates and their embassies, sealed letters might be sent subject to the right of the military commander to stop sealed correspondence in zones where military movements were taking place.

The American consul at Swansea, Wales, reported on December 11, 1914, the receipt of a letter from the German department of the American embassy which bore evidence of having been broken open by the censor. So also the American consul at Amsterdam on December 17, 1914, reported the receipt of a letter which had been opened by the British censor. The American legation at the Hague wrote the consul that a letter had just been received from Ambassador Page in London to the effect that "letters addressed by this or any other mission to consuls or by consuls to any American diplomatic mission are unopened, but correspondence addressed by consuls to others than diplomatic missions are liable to be opened by the censor. This matter has been referred to the Department of State at Washington, who agree with the British Government that consular correspondence is not exempted from the operations of the censors." In reply to the consul the Department of State simply quoted the instructions of April 23, 1915, set out above.

British censorship regulations permitted only messages between diplomatic missions and the Government at Washington to go in cipher. Consequently, a cipher message from the American ministry at Peking to the consul general at Hong Kong was held up until released by special instructions from the British Government.

The British regulations covering telegraph messages recognized the right of neutral Governments to employ diplomatic officers and consuls of career to carry despatches. The foreign office reported on August 2, 1914, that the privilege of sending telegrams in code or cipher would not be extended to consular officers.

Consular correspondence was regarded by the British as being liable to censorship, even to letters from consular officers to a governmental department of the appointing state. In actual practice, however, official correspondence to or from American consular officers in the United Kingdom and to and from allied and American consuls general in neutral countries were exempted from censorship.

The German general staff on November 21, 1916, informed the American consul at Ghent that direct communication by letter between consuls and with the diplomatic representatives recognized by the Belgium Government and located in German controlled territory was forbidden. The despatch containing this information was merely acknowledged and filed by the Department.

The American ambassador at Constantinople on December 1, 1916, protested to the Minister of Foreign Affairs because of a discrimination made against American consular officers in that Austrian, German, and Bulgarian consuls were permitted to send telegrams in cipher and correspondence under seal to their diplomatic missions. The ministry promised an inquiry.

Several cases involving consular correspondence arose during the American civil war. A request from the British minister for information relative to the seizure of the despatch bag of a British vice consul was met with the statement that there was nothing on the bag to indicate that it had come from the vice consul. Suspicious circumstances surrounding the seizure of the bag (the bearer had disappeared at seizure) led to the opening of the bag. All apparently official contents were forwarded to the British legation, others—nature not indicated except that they were such that no vice consul had the right to forward from a place in rebel territory—were retained. *Foreign Relations,* 1861, pp. 174-176.

A further protest on the violation of consular mail brought from Secretary of State Seward on April 5, 1862, the fullest approval of the inviolability of the consular pouch and its contents when under seal. *Foreign Relations,* 1862, p. 258; see also p. 517.

A request from the French ministry that an order be given to facilitate the exchange of official correspondence between the French legation and the French consul at Richmond was passed on to the Secretary of War, with a request for favorable consideration. The latter, however, on the advice of his general-in-chief, found compliance with the request impossible. *Ibid.,* p. 430.

Chile as a neutral in the world war forbade the transmission of telegrams in cipher. Telegrams of diplomatic and consular agents were excepted on the principle of reciprocity. *International Law Situations,* 1916, p. 21.

Provisions for the treatment of consuls of warring nations are very rare. The statement in the *Swedish Consular*

*Ordinance and Instructions* that in the event of war consuls should remain at their posts until otherwise ordered by the Minister of Foreign Affairs or until the exequatur had been revoked is distinctly an exception. Rule 313.

When the German forces occupied a large part of Belgium, the German Government notified states whose consuls had offices in the occupied area that exequaturs granted by the Belgian Government had expired. Belgium protested, as did the Netherlands and Switzerland. The Netherlands protest contained the following language:

The Royal Government does not think that occupation voids the exequaturs of foreign consuls. It admits that military authority may not recognize consuls and may oppose their performing their functions.

The situation of foreigners in Belgium (the frequent need of identification papers, etc.) makes consular assistance at present more useful than ever; events have proved this; since the beginning of the war it has been necessary to station consular officers at Louvain, Charleroi, Dinant, Namur where there were none.

By reason of the lack of means of communications the mails from Brussels, Antwerp, and Liege can reach but a small part of the occupied territory.

The Royal Government is convinced that the Imperial Government, realizing this situation, will not embarrass the consuls now in office, those at Ghent and Bruges particularly being indispensable.

As regards the hope expressed by Germany that the representatives will observe absolute neutrality, the Royal Government will not fail to take action on any complaint or remark that may be laid before it.

The position of the American Government, however, was that " in view of the fact that consular officers are commercial and not political representatives of the Government, and that permission for them to act within defined districts is dependent upon the authority which is in actual control of such districts, irrespective of the question of legal right, and, further, in view of the fact that the consular districts to which reference is made in the Note Verbale of the Imperial Government are within the territory now under German military occupation [the Government of the United States], is not inclined at this time to question the right of the Imperial Government to suspend the exequaturs of the consular officers of the United States within the districts which are occupied by the military forces of the German Empire and subject to its military jurisdiction." *AJIL* Supplement, 1916, pp. 445-459.

The United States embassies at London and Berlin made arrangements for the exchange of British consuls in Germany and German consuls in Great Britain. German consuls of career in England had been permitted to leave freely at the outbreak of the war. Other consuls were exchanged on a man-for-man basis for British consuls in Germany, individual private British citizens being released by Germany to counterbalance the larger number of consular officers in Great Britain and its colonies. *British and Foreign State Papers* CX, pp. 566-611.

Foreign consuls in England were required to register in accordance with the Aliens Restriction Order when residing in a prohibited district, according to a telegram from the consul general at London on November 30, 1914.

The American vice consul at Cologne requested an exemption from the general ordinance which required all aliens not less than eight hours before departure nor more than eight hours after arrival in the area of the eighth army corps to report to the police authorities of the police precinct with passport and a statement of the purpose of the journey and place of destination. The vice consul felt that such restriction would seriously limit his actions within his consular district. The German military authorities refused to grant the exemption requested, pointing out that the ordinance applied to all consular officers. To this the vice consul answered that all of the other consular officers in the district with the exception of the Austro-Hungarian consul general were German and were not subject to this ordinance, and that the Austro-Hungarian consul had stated that he did not know of the existence of the ordinance. The foreign office replied that no exemptions could be made because of the urgency of the war; and the matter was dropped. Ambassador to Germany to Secretary of State, Oct. 11, 1915, with accompanying documents.

## BIBLIOGRAPHY


Albertini, Luis Eugenio, *Derecho Diplomático en sus Aplicaciones Especiales á Las Repúblicas Sud-Americanas.* Paris, 1866.

Allué Salvador, Miguel, *La Condición Jurídica de los Cónsules.* Zaragoza, 1909.

Alvarez, Alexandre, *Le Droit International Américain.*

Antokoletz, Daniel, "La Condición Jurídica de los Cónsules y especialmente de los Cónsules Argentinos" in *Revista Diplomática y Consular Argentina,* Dec., 1915, vol. i, no. 2. Buenos Aires.

Argentina

*Memoria del Ministerio de Relaciones Esteriores.* Buenos Aires, 1879, 1917-1918, 1919-1920.

*Reglamento para los Cónsules Argentinos y Disposiciones Vigentes Relativas al Servicio Consular.* Buenos Aires, 1899.

*Ley No. 4712 de 29 de Septiembre de 1905 sobre Organización del Cuerpo Consular Argentino y Decreto Reglamentario de la Misma de 25 de Enero de 1906.* Buenos Aires, 1906.

*Anuario del Ministerio de Relaciones Exteriores y Culto de la República Argentina.* Buenos Aires, 1908.

Barcelo, D. Simon, *Manual Diplomático y Consular Hispano-Americano.* Barcelona, 1909.

Barros, Julio Zentano, *Servicio Diplomático i Consular: Lejislación Vijente en 1896.* Santiago, 1896.

Bequet, Léon, *Répertoire de Droit Administratif.* 24v. Paris, 1882.

Bertheau, Hippolyte, *Dictionnaire Général de Droit et de Jurisprudence.* Paris, n. d.

Bodin, Albert, *Des Immunités Consulaires dans les Pays de Chrétienté.* Bordeaux, 1897.

Bolivia

*Reglamento Consular de la República de Bolivia.* La Paz, 1877.

*Informe del Ministerio de Relaciones Exteriores y Culto al Congreso Ordinario de 1890.* La Paz, 1890.

Borel, François, *De l'Origine et des Fonctions des Consuls.* St. Pétersbourg, 1807.

Bursotti, Giovanni, *Guide des Agents Consulaires.* 2v. Naples, 1838.

Bustos L., Emiliano, i Montane U, Augusto, *Lejislación Diplomática i Consular de Chile.* Santiago, 1916.

Calvo, Charles

*Le Droit International Théorique et Pratique.* 5th ed. 6v. Paris, 1896.

*Dictionnaire de Droit International Public et Privé.* 2v. Paris and Berlin, 1885.

*Dictionnaire Manuel de Diplomatie et de Droit International.* Paris and Berlin, 1885.

Carette, Augusto, *Diccionario de la Jurisprudencia Argentina.* 3v. Buenos Aires, 1907, 1910, 1912.

de Castro y Casaleiz, Antonio, *Guía Practica del Diplomático Español.* 2v. Madrid, 1886.

Chevrey-Rameau, Paul, *Répertoire Diplomatique et Consulaire.* Paris, 1883.

Chile

*Manual del Marino*, vol. i (1888), vol. ix (1899). Santiago.

*Memoria del Ministro de Relaciones Esteriores.* 1896. Santiago.

*Boletín de Relaciones Esteriores*, 1914, no. 42. Santiago.

*Servicio Consular de la República de Chile.* Santiago, 1897.

de Clerq, Alex. and de Vallat, C., *Guide des Consulats.* 3v. Paris, 1898.

Cobbett, Pitt, *Leading Cases on International Law*, 4th ed. 2v. London, 1922.

Colombia

*Constitución Política de Colombia, Actos Legislativos que la Reforman, y Leyes de 1905.* Bogotá, 1905.

*Guía Consular de la República de Colombia.* Bogotá, 1907.

*Memoria del Ministerio de Relaciones Esteriores al Congreso.* Bogotá, 1914.

Costa Rica

*Reglamento Consular de 1° de Noviembre de 1881.* 2d ed. San José, 1888.

*La Gaceta—Diario Oficial*, May 7, 1920, "Ley Orgánica del Servicio Consular." San José.

Cuba

*Compilación de Decretos del Sr. Presidente y de Circulares y Consultas del Departmento Referentes al Servicio Diplomático y Consular.* Habana, 1904.

*Instrucciones Provisionales para el Servicio Consular.* Habana, 1904.

*Ley Orgánica del Servicio Diplomático y Consular de la República de Cuba.* Habana, 1903.

*Leyes Políticas y Decretos referentes á la Representación Diplomática y Consular de la República de Cuba.* Habana, 1903.

de Cussy, Baron Ferdinand

*Dictionnaire ou Manuel-lexique du Diplomate et du Consul.* Leipzig, 1846.

*Règlements Consulaires des Principaux États Maritimes de l'Europe et de l'Amérique.* Leipzig, 1851.

Delepoule, Eugène, *Exposé Théorique de la Fiction d'Exterritorialité par Rapport aux Personnes en Droit International Public.* Paris, 1897.

Denmark

*Instructions pour les Consuls de Danemark à l'Étranger.* Copenhagen, 1894.

*Danish Consular Instructions of January 18, 1912.* Copenhagen, 1912.

Dietrich, Victor, *De l'Inviolabilité et de l'Exemption de Juridiction des Agents Diplomatiques et Consulaires en Pays de Chrétienté.* Paris, 1896.

Dominican Republic, *Ley Orgánica del Cuerpo Consular de la República Dominicana, 25 de Julio de 1887.* Santo Domingo, 1915.

Droin, Ceser, *L'Exterritorialité des Agents Diplomatiques.* Geneva, 1895.

Ecuador

*Ley que Reglamenta el Servicio Consular.* Quito, 1898.

*Ley y Decretos Legislativos y Ejecutivos Relacionados con el Servicio Diplomático y Consular del Ecuador.* Quito, 1909.

*Leyes, Decretos Legislativos y Ejecutivos Reglamentos . . . Relacionados con el Servicio Diplomático y Consular del Ecuador.* Quito, 1917.

Esriche, Joaquin, *Diccionario Razonado de Legislación y Jurisprudencia.* Madrid, 1874.

*Enciclopedia Jurídica Española.* Barcelona, 1910 with annual supplements.

Finland, *Décret Contenant le Statut des Légations et des Consulats.* Helsinki/Helsingfors, 1919.

Fiore, Pasquale, *International Law Codified.* Translated from the fifth Italian edition by E. M. Borchard. New York, 1918.

Fynn, Robert, *British Consuls Abroad.* London, 1846.

Garcia de la Vega, *Guide Pratique des Agents Politiques de Ministre des Affaires Étrangères de Belgique.* 4th ed. Paris, 1899.

Garcia Salazar, Arturo, y Linch, Jorge, *Guía Práctica para los Diplomáticos y Cónsules Peruanos.* Lima, 1918.

de Garden, Guillaume (Un Ancien Ministre), *Traité Complet de Diplomatie.* 3v. Paris, 1833.

Garner, James Wilford, *International Law and the World War.* London, 1920.

Germany, *General Instructions for Consuls of the German Empire of the 6. June 1871.* Translated by Charles Kirchhoff. New York, 1872.

Great Britain

*Reports relative to British Consular Establishments: 1858 & 1871.* 2v. London, 1872.

*British and Foreign State Papers.* 113v for the years 1812-1920 London, 1841-1923.

Greece, *Code Consulaire*. Athens, 1918.

Guatemala, *Reglamento Diplomático y Consular de la República de Guatemala*. Guatemala, 1900.

Guesalaga, Alejandro, *Derecho Diplomático y Consular con los Últimos Casos de Controversias entre los Estados*. Buenos Aires, 1900.

Hawaii

*General Instructions for His Majesty's Consuls*. Honolulu, 1880.

*Regulations for the Consular Service of the Republic of Hawaii*. Honolulu, 1895.

Henshaw, Joshua Sidney, *A Manual for United States Consuls*. New York, 1849.

Heyking, Baron Alfons Alfonsovich, *A Practical Guide for Russian Consular Officers and Private Persons Having Relations with Russia*. London, 1904. 2d. ed., 1916.

Honduras

*Reglamento Consular*. Tegucigalpa, 1906.

*Ley sobre Misiones Consulares Extranjeras*. Tegucigalpa, 1906.

Hyde, Charles Cheney, *International Law: Chiefly as Interpreted and Applied by the United States*. 2v. Boston, 1922.

International Law Association, *Report of the Thirty-First Conference Held at the Palace of Justice, Buenos Aires, 24th August–30th August, 1922*. London, 1923.

Jamar, Lucien

*Répertoire Général de la Jurisprudence Belge 1814-1880*. Bruxelles, 1883.

*Répertoire Decennal de la Jurisprudence Belge 1890 à 1900*. Bruxelles, n. d.

Keim, Benneville Randolph, *A Report to the Honorable George S. Boutwell, Secretary of the Treasury, upon the Condition of the Consular Service of the United States of America*. Washington, 1872.

Kent, James, *Commentaries on American Law*. 3d edition. New York, 1836.

Laget de Podio, *Nouvelle Juridiction des Consuls de France à l'Étranger*. Marseille, 1844. 2d ed.

Larrainzar, Frederico, *Los Consulados*. Mexico, 1874.

Larrive, Georges, *Les Privilèges des Consuls dans les Pays d'Occident*. Paris, 1901.

Lehr, Ernest, *Manuel Théorique et Pratique des Agents Diplomatiques et Consulaires Français et Étrangers*. Paris, 1888.

Leroy, Paul, *Des Consulats des Légations et des Ambassades: Étude d'Histoire et de Droit*. 2d ed. Paris, 1876.

Liberia, *Consular Regulations of the Republic of Liberia*. Monrovia, 1906.

Ludwig, Ernest, *Consular Treaty Rights*. Akron, 1913.

Louter, J. de, *Le Droit International Public Positif.* 2v. Oxford, 1920.

Madiedo, Manuel Maria, *Tratado de Derecho de Jentes, Internacional, Diplomático i Consular.* Bogotá, 1874.

Malloy, W. M., *Treaties, Conventions, International Acts, Protocols, and Agreements between the United States of America and Other Powers.* 2v. Washington, 1910. Third Supplementary Volume, 1924.

Maluquer y Salvador, Miguel, *Derecho Consular Español,* Madrid, 1899 with appendices of 1901 and 1908.

de Martens, Baron Charles

*Causes Célèbres du Droit des Gens.* 2d ed. 5v. Leipzig, 1861.

*Le Guide Diplomatique.* 5th ed. 2v. Leipzig, 1866.

de Mensch, Friedrich August, *Manuel Pratique de Consulat: Ouvrage Consacré spécialmente aux Consuls de Prusse.* Leipzig, 1846.

Mexico

*Derecho Internacional Mexicano.* 3v. Mexico, 1879.

*Reglamento del Cuerpo Consular Mexicano.* Mexico, 1878.

*Guía Diplomática y Consular.* Mexico, 1902.

*Guía Consular.* Mexico, 1905.

*Ley Orgánica y Reglamento del Servicio Consular Mexicano.* Mexico, 1911.

*Reglamento de la Ley Orgánica del Servicio Consular Mexicano.* Mexico, 1924.

Moore, John Bassett

*Asylum in Legations and Consulates.* New York, 1892.

*Digest of International Law.* 8v. Washington, 1906.

de Moreuil, L.-J.-A., *Dictionnaire des Chancelleries Diplomatiques et Consulaires.* 2v. Paris, 1855.

Moreuil, M., *Manuel des Agents Consulaires Français et Étrangers.* Paris, 1850.

Morse, Alexander Porter, *The So-called Right of Asylum in Legations.* Albany, 1892.

Netherlands

*Netherlands Consular Instructions.* The Hague, 1889.

*Ibid.*, 1902.

*Netherlands Consular Service Rules and Regulations 1908.* Amsterdam, 1908.

Nicaragua

*Reglamento del Servicio Consular de Nicaragua emitido en 16 Octubre de 1880.* Managua, 1893.

*Ley Consular.* Managua, 1904.

Ordenez Lopez, Manuel, *Constitución Política de la República de Bolivia; Leyes y Disposiciones Más Usuales.* La Paz, 1917.

Ozanam, Charles, *L'Immunité Civile de Juridiction des Agents Diplomatiques.* Paris, 1912.

Palau, Lisimaco, *Guía para los Cónsules Colombianos.* 3d ed. Bogotá, 1893.

Panama

*Leyes y Decretos Vigentes en la República de Panama sobre los Servicios Diplomático y Consular.* Panama, 1913.

*Leyes y Decretos sobre Servicio Consular.* Panama, 1916.

*Disposiciones Consulares Vigentes en la República de Panama.* Panama, 1918.

Paraguay

*Regulations for the Consuls of the Republic of Paraguay.* Philadelphia, 1901.

*Reglamento Consular.* Asuncion, 1913.

Patau, Paul, *De la Situation Comparée des Agents Diplomatiques et Consulaires.* Toulouse, 1910.

Perez-Sarmiento, Jose Manuel, *Manual Consular Colombiano.* Cadiz, 1913.

Persia, *Règlement des Consulats de Perse.* Teheran, 1901.

Peru

*Reglamento del Servicio Consular del Peru.* Lima, 1874.

*Reglamento Consular del Peru.* Lima, 1912.

Pinheiro-Ferreira, Silvestre, *Observations sur le Guide Diplomatique de M. le Baron Ch. de Martens.* Paris, 1837.

Pradier-Fodere, Paul Louis Ernest, *Cours de Droit Diplomatique.* 2d ed. 2v. Paris, 1899.

Price, Hannibal, *Dictionnaire de Législation Administrative Haitienne.* Port-au-Prince, 1923.

Ramirez Peña, Abraham, *Cartilla Consular.* San Salvador, 1916.

Raynelli, Ernesto T., *Derecho Diplomático Moderno.* Buenos Aires, 1914.

de Rosa Rullo, Gabriel, *Code-Mémorial International & Maritime des Consulats.* Naples, 1902.

Ruiz, Carlos Castro, i Mora, Luis R., *Lejislación Diplomática i Consular de Chile.* Valparaiso, 1912.

Salles, Georges, *L'Institution des Consulats: Son Origine, son Développement au Moyen-Age Chez les Différents Peuples.* Paris, 1898.

Salvador

*Ley Orgánica del Cuerpo Diplomático y Consular.* San Salvador, 1905.

*Ley sobre Misiones Consulares Extranjeras.* San Salvador, 1905.

*Recopilación de Disposiciones Relativas al Ramo Consular Salvadoreño.* San Salvador, 1915.

Saravia, Antonio Gonzalez, *Derecho Patrio.* Guatemala, 1910.

Scott, James Brown, ed., *Resolutions of the Institute of International Law.* Washington,

Seijas, Raphael F., *El Derecho Internacional Hispano-Americano.* 6v. Caracas, 1884.

South African Republic, *Regulations for Consular Officers of the South African Republic in Foreign Parts.* Pretoria, 1895.

Spain, *Guía Diplomática y Consular de España.* Madrid, 1908.

Stowell, Ellery C.

*Le Consul.* Paris, 1909.

*Consular Cases and Opinions.* Washington, 1909.

*The Magee Incident.* Washington, 1920.

Stowell, Ellery C. and Munro, Henry F., *International Cases.* 2v. Boston, 1916.

Sweden, *Royal Ordinance concerning the Consular Service of Sweden . . . and General Instructions.* Stockholm, 1909.

Switzerland, *Règlement Consulaire Suisse.* Berne, 1924.

Texas, *General Instructions for the Government of the Consular and Commercial Agents of the Republic of Texas.* Houston, 1838.

Toda y Guell, Eduardo, *Derecho Consular de España.* Madrid, 1889.

de la Torre y Reine, Raphael, *Manual de Derecho Consular Cubano.* Habana, 1918.

Tuson, E. W. A., *British Consul's Manual.* London, 1856.

United States

Congress

Sen. Ex. Doc. No. 31, Vol. 9, 36th Cong., 1st ses.

H. Ex. Doc. No. 39, Vol. 9, 38th Cong., 1st ses.

Sen. Ex. Doc. No. 40, Vol. 2, 40th Cong., 2d ses.

H. Misc. Doc. No. 189, 42d Cong., 2d ses.

H. Ex. Doc. No. 317, 42d Cong., 2d ses.

Sen. Rept. No. 1302, 56th Cong., 1st ses.

Department of State.

*Consular Instructions.* Washington.

*Standing Instructions to Consuls and Vice-Consuls of the United States.* Washington, 1805.

*Ibid.* 1815.

*Message from the President of the United States in Relation to the Consular Establishment of the United States.* 1833.

*General Instructions to the Consuls and Commercial Agents of the United States.* 1833.

*Consular Regulations.* 1868.

*Regulations Prescribed for the Use of the Consular Service of the United States.* 1870.

*Ibid.* 1874.

*Ibid.* 1881.

*Ibid.* 1888.

*Ibid.* 1896.

*Regulations Governing the Consular Service of the United States (annotated to December 31, 1922).* 1923.
*Regulations to Govern Transportation of Diplomatic and Consular Officers.* 1919.
*Papers relating to the Foreign Relations of the United States.* 81v. for the years 1861-1916. 1861-1926.
Department of the Navy
*Naval War College Publications.*
Department of the Treasury
*Treasury Decisions.* (Several volumes per year.)
*General Regulations under the Customs and Navigation Laws of the United States.* 1884.
*Customs Regulations.* 1923.
Uribe, Antonio José, *Anales Diplomáticos y Consulares de Colombia.* 6v. Bogotá, 1904-1920.
Uruguay
*Reglamento por el cual Deben Regirse los Cónsules de la República Oriental del Uruguay en el Ejercicio de sus Funciones.* Montevideo, 1878.
*Ibid. Reformado con la Ley del 12 Mayo del Año 1884.*
*Leyes de Organización Diplomática y Consular.* Montevideo, 1907.
*Memoria del Ministerio de Relaciones Exteriores.* 1914-1915.
*Leyes de Organización y de Arancel Consulares.* Montevideo, 1918, with supplements to 1920.
Vades, Manuel M., *Guía del Cónsul Panameño.* Bruxelles, 1912.
Venegas, Florencio A., *Lejislación Consular de la República de Chile.* 2v. Santiago, 1909.
Venezuela
*Ley de 31 de Mayo de 1887 sobre Servicio Consular de los Estados Unidos de Venezuela.* Caracas, 1887.
*Ley sobre Servicio Consular de los Estados Unidos de Venezuela.* Caracas, 1910.
*Gaceta Oficial,* June 28, 1912.
*Ibid.,* Sept. 29, 1923.
*Ley Orgánica del Servicio Consular de los Estados Unidos de Venezuela con un Apéndice Contentive de las Leyes, Decretos, y Resoluciones sobre la Materia.* Caracas, 1921.
*El Libro Amarillo de los Estados Unidos de Venezuela.* Caracas, 1923.
Vera, Robustiano, *Manual para Diplomáticos y Cónsules.* Santiago, 1909.
Verge, Jacques, *Des Consuls dans les Pays d'Occident.* Paris, 1903.
de Vivero, Domingo, *Guía Diplomático y Consular del Peru.* Lima, 1889.
Weiss, Andre
*Répertoire des Pandectes Françaises.* Paris, 1896.
*Supplement au Répertoire des Pandectes Françaises.* Paris, 1908.

Wertheim, Johzn., *Manuel à l'Usage des Consuls des Pays-Bas.* 3v. Amsterdam, 1861.

Wharton, Francis, *Digest of International Law.* 3v. Washington, 1887.

Wheaton, Henry, *Elements of International Law.* Dana's edition, Boston, 1866.

de Wicquefort, Abraham, *The Embassador and his Functions.* Translated by John Digby. London, n. d.

Zegarra, Felix Cipriano C., *La Condición Jurídica de los Extranjeros en el Peru.* Santiago, 1872.

# INDEX